T0146896

WELL WATER:
NOT MY REAL NAME

WELL WATER:
NOT MY REAL NAME

*The Psychological Effects of Racism on
African-American Children*

The Need to Understand Change

DANNY E. BLANCHARD

Copyright © 2014 by Danny E. Blanchard.

Library of Congress Control Number:		2014919961
ISBN:	Hardcover	978-1-5035-1383-9
	Softcover	978-1-5035-1384-6
	eBook	978-1-5035-1382-2

All rights reserved. No part of this book may be reproduced or transmitted in any form or by any means, electronic or mechanical, including photocopying, recording, or by any information storage and retrieval system, without permission in writing from the copyright owner.

Any people depicted in stock imagery provided by Thinkstock are models, and such images are being used for illustrative purposes only.
Certain stock imagery © Thinkstock.

This book was printed in the United States of America.

Rev. date: 02/02/2015

To order additional copies of this book, contact:
Xlibris
1-888-795-4274
www.Xlibris.com
Orders@Xlibris.com
603271

DEDICATION

Lola Brown M.D. M.B.A.

My faithful confidant, my dearest friend, and my loving companion.

May God continue to bless you and your medical care for all children.

ACKNOWLEDGEMENTS

I owe a debt of gratitude to these individuals:

Justine Revelle (editor and reader), Alicia Angland (editor and reader), Chammand Deesanit (reader), Mervyn A. Warren PhD, D. Min.; Raymond A. Winbush PhD

Their wisdom, motivation, encouragement, time and interest in my writings helped make possible the publishing of this book.

TABLE OF CONTENTS

WELL WATER: NOT MY REAL NAME

THE PSYCHOLOGICAL EFFECTS OF RACISM ON AFRICAN-AMERICAN CHILDREN

AUTHOR'S NOTES

After writing this book, I feel that it says a lot about my own upbringing and development in Redlands, California. It is a genuine reflection of that which I, along with many friends and mentors, no longer with me, experienced. This book gives a clear understanding on how racism affects a child; be he or she black, white or Hispanic American. I learned very early in my childhood that racism is a disease. Only through a proper diagnosis and treatment can it be cured. How utterly unfair it is to have to experience this disease at such an early age.

As you read this book, I hope that you will discover insights and principles that will help all children gain strength, hope, confidence, courage, and positive relationship with God.

The key to close and lock the doors of racism and its effects on children lies within our spiritual and educational institutions. It is within their walls that change and deliverance will occur.

Follow my research and learn.

WELL WATER: NOT MY REAL NAME
THE PSYCHOLOGICAL EFFECTS OF RACISM ON
AFRICAN-AMERICAN CHILDREN

WELL WATER: NOT MY REAL NAME
THE PSYCHOLOGICAL EFFECTS OF RACISM ON AFRICAN-AMERICAN CHILDREN

Little has been said or written concerning the children of the slave trade. Follow me to Africa, at the height of the slave trade, as I share the misfortunes of a family victimized by this horrific moment in time. Although fictitious, it will bring insight regarding what many African children experienced during this most unusual period of world history.

WELL WATER: NOT MY REAL NAME

The journey starts in Africa…

Let us now begin this journey together from Africa. Hope remains, that in spite of horrific challenges faced by African-American children, life will become more meaningful, healthy, successful, motivational, and educational as they grow and develop.

"Well Water"

Her name was Well Water; but not her birth name. This was the name her slave masters gave this 12-year-old princess from the Continent of Africa. She was captured at the height of the slave trade in 1802 by slavers from the Louisiana Coast in Southern America.

Well Water hid from slavers during a raid on her father and mother's camp in Africa. Well Water was an excellent swimmer and runner with beautiful black hair. She was known for her ability to outrun and out swim all the boys and girls in her village. Her father, Naifissa Obieue was a Montego warrior and a prince. Her mother Shariffe Obieue was a beautiful princess. She had a younger 11-year-old brother who was a strong hunter and considered to be the best in the village for his age. His name was Naifissa Obieue, named after his father. Well Water's real name was Sagifie Obieue, named after her mother. She came from a strong intelligent family. For the Oblique's family was the most important value. Sagifie was well aware of slavery and its brutality. She heard the stories from her father and the other villagers. This made her very much aware of the evils of slavery. She was taught how to protect herself from the white slave hunters who came to her country in great large ships to capture people from various tribes and take them far away, never to be seen again. She and her brother would always play together along with other children from the village, but never alone.

The trees and tall brush were easy to hide in along the coast of their village home where hunting and fishing was bountiful. The children of the village were not allowed to play outside at night because no one ever knew when the white man would come with his weapons of smoke and fire, from his ships, and take people away. No one ever came back to the tribes to tell what happened to them, or to tell of their experiences. There were stories of other tribes who would sell their friends and enemies to the slave catchers for gold and silver.

Sagifie was always told by her parents that her name and family were the two most important values in her life. Her parents emphasized that she should always keep the family and its name above all else, and never let anyone take them from her. Her father often spoke about this with all of the village children; he would never let them forget it. Rumors spread around villages that more big ships were spotted and more would be coming. Word spread that many people were taken aboard ships never to be seen again.

One day, Sagifie's father decided to move his family further inland away from the coast. The decision was made primarily for safety and security. Naifissa would often speak to the other warriors about how they should defend their homes and families if they were attacked, or if slavers ever tried to capture them. Tribal meetings were held on a regular basis, which included discussions on ways that tribes and villages could be protected from white slavers.

Sagifie always wondered why men from other parts of the world would come to their country and want to harm them. Stealing, killing, and burning their villages seemed so strange and peculiar. Why would people who confessed to know God acts like savages? Her father would always say that they, the slavers, were the savages and the evil ones. He would often say that they were too lazy to tend to their own work and fields, so they had to get other people, who they hated, to do their work.

Sagifie had a very pleasing personality and was loved by all within the village. She would often teach the other children in the village how to swim and hunt small game. Her mother taught her how to cook and sharpen her skills. Warnings became more frequent as messengers from other villages reported hundreds of big ships were being aligned up and down the coast of the villages. Sagifie's father decided to move the family even further into the interior of the country. The men from the big ships carried weapons of smoke and fire which were more powerful than her father's spears and arrows. Moving every six to twelve months began to take a toll on the family. At one point Sagifie overheard her father speak to the other warriors about attacking the men from the big ships at night, burning their ships, and killing all of the white men who were with them.

Many nights, Sagifie feared that she and her family would be taken away by these evil men. She would often sleep with knives and spears in her hut. Guards were spread across the villages at night. They used warning signs and made loud animal noises to let the villages know that the slave catchers were near. At times, Sagifie could smell the campfires of the slave catchers and knew that at any day they could attack. Once, she actually saw a white man hunting game about a mile from her village. He ran after her with a large net, but Sagifie was too fast for him. She told her father what had happened. Her father and the other warriors went looking for this fat, bald-headed, bearded white man, as described by Sagifie. However, he was gone by the time they surrounded his camp. As a result of this incident, Sagifie's father began having more tribal meetings. More security was placed around the outer perimeter of the village and more warriors were put on full alert. Women and children were instructed not to go very far. Hunting and fishing would no longer be done unless warriors were with each individual group. More and more messengers from the other villages were telling stories about raids, kidnappings, and rape. Many villages had been burned to the ground by the white men from the big ships.

Stories were told about how groups of people were being chained and beaten as they were moved to the ships never to be seen again. Many were marched down the coast, vanished, or never survived the journey. Others were simply left to die. Stories were told about how many captured Africans would eat the dirt as they were dragged to the ships. This was done to remember their homeland and to take part of it with them as they boarded the ships. Pregnant women were often killed and left at sea because they were too much of a burden aboard the ships. Stories were told about how slaves would kill themselves and their children, rather than board the slave ships. Others would kill their small children before they arrived on the ship. Women and men were often raped while waiting to board the big ships. Many messengers indicated that nothing could be done to save or help them. White men would be seen drinking strange liquids which would make them act crazy and dizzy. At times, they would become enraged and attack each other while in a drunken stupor.

"It made no difference who would be captured," the messengers would say. Princesses, princes, kings, craftsman, cooks, warriors, hunters, queens, and many children from various villages that spoke different languages, all were taken aboard the big ships. Some women and young girls were being raped by as many as 1 0 - 15 slavers at a time. Some warriors and villagers who were captured had a broken arm or an eye plucked out if they caused any problems while boarding the ships or at sea. They were beaten with clubs and sustained broken legs and arms as they boarded the big ships. Sagifie's father was extremely angry to hear of such stories given by the messengers. He was determined to protect his children at all costs.

One warm evening, Sagifie's family heard very loud popping sounds around the villages. Sagifie's mother grabbed her brother and they all started to run as far as possible into the back of the village. They got about 1 00 yards into the woods where they were met by four white men with nets and steel metal looking claws. Her mother and brother cried as the white men threw nets over them and bound their hands and feet as though they were animals. The family was made to walk like captured wild animals from the jungle. They were taken back to the center of the village. Many of their friends were covered with nets and shackles like animals. As Sagifie looked around for her father, she saw him and other warriors being beaten and shackled with steel braces around their necks.

Sagifie's father looked at her with fear in his eyes. He whispered over and over to her, "Remember your name and family, Sagifie." They soon found themselves being marched to the ocean. Many men, women and children from different tribes were being taken to the ocean. They were either naked or wore rags for clothing. Those who could not make the journey to the ocean were left to die, or thrown into the ocean like bad fish. Although he was shackled and netted, Sagifie watched as her little brother attempted to run away. He was hit with a big wooden club and his elbow appeared to be dislocated. As he yelled in pain, her father mustered up all of his strength, broke the net that had him bound, and ran to her brother. He hit three large white men, grabbed her little brother, and held him to his chest. He was soon subdued and beaten until he was unconscious. He could no longer move. Sagifie's mother had already been carried away to the big ship with the other women. Sagifie had watched her mother as she boarded the ship with her head held high and praying to God Almighty.

As they dragged her father onto the ship, Sagifie heard a white man say, "Hurt him no more. He's worth more money with less injuries." Her little brother was placed with the other male children as they were herded like sheep up the wooden rail onto the ship. Sagifie's little brother looked up at her and his lips moved to say, "Remember your name and your family." He then disappeared.

The young women were made to strip naked to be examined by the ship's crew. Some took the young girls to their cabins; only God knew what happened to them on their journey. Altogether they numbered 300 women, 500 men and about 50 children. Sagifie wondered how they could place everyone on that one ship. She soon learned that they would be closely packed in a large dark hole at the bottom of this ship. The smell of vomit, urine, and feces was everywhere. The smell made her very dizzy and ill. She continued to hear loud moans, crying, screaming, and praying.

Sagifie needed fresh clean water, but so did everyone else at the bottom of the hellish ship. How could these people be so wicked? The crew called them black savages who were only there to serve the white man. The truth is they were the real savages. They burned their homes, raped and killed, and sold them into slavery. Sagifie didn't understand how this can occur. She thought to herself, why would these people want to destroy a land they know nothing about? They were children of a prosperous land, but now their homeland was cursed by the evils of the white man's slavery.

Herded into the bottom of the ship like animals, Sagifie and her brother lost sight of each other. Their mother was bunked in a different section of the ship. She believed her father, mother, and brother were dead or were going to die. As Sagifie lay at the bottom of the ship, she felt it begin to move as the ocean waters began to slap alongside the great vessel. The chains made terrible and frightening sounds from the bottom of the ship as it slowly moved. Sagifie felt her body splitting in half as she began to vomit the food she was fed. She thought about how long they would be down there and if the madness would ever end. They must have stayed at the bottom of the ship for at least six nights and seven days before they were brought up for fresh air, exercise and water. The white man threw seawater all over their bodies causing everyone to yell. Sagifie saw her mother and father were ill from the beatings they had received. For some reason, her little brother was standing by their mother. He had scars all over his body from an apparent beating as well. Sagifie watched her mother crying and her father moving his lips towards her.

When he finally got the words out, "Do not forget your name Sagifie," a large whip was cracked across his face. Sagifie watched as the blood gushed out and ran down his face like a tiny river. Her father became so angry that he hit the slaver with his hand and broke the man's jaw and nose. The other warriors that were hooked up to the chains also got into the fight. Fighting broke out everywhere. She saw her father run over to her mother and brother. She ran towards them while the fighting continued. Sagifie's father, brother, and mother leapt over into the ocean. She tried to jump in the ocean to be with them, but a slaver threw a wooden club at her just as she was about to join her parents in the ocean to die. Blood trickle-down into Sagifie's eyes, so she could no longer see. From the ocean, Sagifie heard her parents say, "Do not forget your name Sagifie, do not forget your name." Their cries became faint as they tried to swim away into the ocean. They were dying and Sagifie wished she could have jumped into the ocean with them. Sagifie knew that when the chance came she would jump into the ocean to die with them. As they came to the New World, Sagifie thought they were back in Africa. However, it was only a dream. When they landed, all of them were taken off the ship. Some were already dead, some sick, some had broken bones, and others were half-starved.

Sagifie was taken off the ship to a wide open space. Many were being sold to the hundreds of slave-owners. They wanted an early bid on the fresh black slave ship. Soon, it was time for Sagifie's turn to be sold. She was stripped naked, touched, pushed, and pulled by white men and women while their black slaves just looked on. Eventually, she was bought by a Frenchman who was married to a white woman. After being washed down by a slave the Frenchwomen owned, they put her into a very fancy coach, clean and tidy. She wore a pair of slave pants and a shirt to cover her body. They rode for miles until they came upon a huge white home with a large field of what she later learned was tobacco and sugar cane. Sagifie soon learned that she was living in New Orleans, in a state called Louisiana, on a plantation by the name of Pointe Louise.

It was the home of a very wealthy landowner and his family. He had three daughters and two sons. She was informed of his rules and given her work assignments. Sagifie was responsible for watching, bathing, and attending to the needs of Master Paroe's three daughters. He never asked Sagifie her name. She was only called Slave Girl or the Girl from Africa. Sagifie was 12 years old, and would soon be 13. She would watch the daughters all day and half the night. She would sleep at the end of the bed, on the floor. She attended to the fires and made sure that all of the master's daughters were cared for and made to feel comfortable. Sagifie was allowed to eat the leftover food from the children's table and she could bathe and change clothes when the master's wife saw fit. She never learned to read and write because it was forbidden.

It was virtually impossible to escape and run away. That was something which was never done or even thought about. A runaway attempt or learning to read and write were actions that the master could never forgive. Sagifie heard of stories about slaves running away and how they would be kicked or beaten in front of other slaves as a warning. There were times that she did not care. Sagifie felt she had nothing to lose or live for. Maybe dying was the best answer, but she remember the words of her father. "Do not forget your name Sagifie; do not forget your name."

One hot day, that master wanted her to take his three daughters to the lake to put their feet and hands in the water. He told her not to go out too deep because they did not know how to swim. The master's 12-year-old daughter jumped into the deep end of the water. She began to yell for help. Sagifie immediately jumped into the lake and swam to save her; she brought her to the shallow part of the lake. She yelled out to the other slaves, working in the fields, for help.

Sagifie saw the girl's father and mother run up to their daughter and put a heavy blanket around her. She told her parents that she had been disobedient and that Sagifie saved her life. As they walked up to the plantation the girl's father and mother hugged Sagifie. Sagifie had never been hugged by white person before. They said she would be receiving a gift for saving their daughter's life. They gave her three little baby pigs and a new blanket. One day, while Sagifie was washing the baby pigs by the big well, her master came to her and said he would give her a new name. "You shall be called, Well Water. Well Water is your new name." She detested the name, but had to answer to it. If not, she would be beaten, or not be fed for a few days at a time.

She started to hear rumors about the north and what was happening to many slaves as they were running away. As they escaped up north, they were given food and shelter along the way. It was called the Underground Railroad. At night, Sagifie would think about being free. Why couldn't she be free? Why was she a slave? What would make a person want to own someone, beat them, rape them, and destroy their whole way of life? They were not the evil savages. Who would treat people like this and be so uncivilized?

Sagifie never accepted her name change. She believed her name was bigger than life and the white man's slavery. Children's dreams were broken and destroyed as a result of slavery. Sagifie's dreams were never fulfilled, and her life ended as a result of untreated pneumonia. She never married, had any children, and never had her taste of freedom. However, she never forgot what her father told her, "Never forget your name." She didn't die with the slave name Well Water, but with her African name Sagifie Obieue. She was a princess from West Africa, the daughter of a great Montego warrior and a beautiful princess. She was a sister to her little baby brother; a small prince.

THE HISTORY OF RACISM AND HOW IT AFFECTS BLACK CHILDREN

As we know the history of African Americans has thus been long and complex in the United States. It is this experience that led to the formation of the present African American identity with all that encompasses in terms of culture, art and literature. Blacks were largely denied opportunities for education and personal advancement until after the Civil Rights Movement.

Racism Defined

Racism is defined as a system of advantage based on race. In America whites have control over resources such as jobs and education. This gives them the power to be racists toward others. Because people of color do not have this power, are not able to be racist towards whites.

Many whites would not consider themselves as racist, but there are different forms of racism. Active racism is what most would consider racist behavior. Active racism is blatant, intentional acts of racial bigotry and discrimination. Today, a more common form of racism is passive racism. Examples of this would be laughing at a racist joke, allowing exclusionary hiring practices go unchallenged, and avoiding difficult race-related issues. Below is a metaphor used to describe these two forms of racism:

Visualize the ongoing cycle of racism as a moving walkway at the airport. Active racist behavior is equivalent to walking fast on the conveyor belt. The person engaged in active racist behavior has identified with the ideology of white supremacy and is moving with it. Passive racist behavior is equivalent to standing still on the walkway. No overt effort is being made, but the conveyor belt moves the bystanders along to the same destination as those who are actively walking. Some of the bystanders may feel the motion of the conveyor belt, see the active racists ahead of them, and choose to turn around, unwilling to go the same destination as the white supremacists. Another form of racism is called cultural racism. This is when the cultural images and messages that affirm the superiority of whites and the assumed inferiority disadvantage people of color. Because racism is so ingrained in the fabric of American institutions, it is easily self-perpetuating; all that is required to maintain it is business as usual.

Connections to Racism: Prejudice and Internalized Racism

Racism exists because of prejudice. Prejudice is defined as a preconceived opinion or judgment, usually based on limited information. If a person's has prejudice attitudes and opinions, they allow it to effect their decisions and actions, creating the racism. Stereotypes, omissions, and distortions all contribute to the development of prejudice, and most of these are found in the media. Prejudice is one of the inescapable consequences of living in a racist society. It is like smog in the air. Sometimes it is so thick it is visible, other times it is less apparent, but always, day in and day out, we are breathing the air in. None of us would introduce ourselves as "smog-breathers" (and most of us don't want to be described as prejudice), but if we live in a smoggy place, how can we avoid the air?

It is the responsibility of all those who are aware of the pollution to clean it up, even if we weren't the ones who polluted the air. It is important that we do not pass prejudice views to our family, friends, or anyone else around us. When you combine "prejudice plus power", you form a strong system of oppression. In my opinion racial prejudice when combined with social power, (access to social, cultural, economic resources and decision-making), it leads to the institutionalization of racist policies and practices. As a result this cycle of prejudice and racism continues.

This cycle of oppression has negative effects, especially on people of color. If a person continuously hears negative messages about his or her racial group, over time they actually start to believe these stereotypes. When people start to internalize these messages, it turns into internalized racism. Internalized racism may have people of color feeling inferior or different because they have come to believe, have internalized, the dominant society's message that they are different and do not belong.

In my opinion the three main effects of internalized racism: The first effect is that internalized racism can generate questions and doubts in the minds of people of color placed in a predominately white setting. Second, internalized racism can lead people of color to question their own thinking and judgment about racism. Third, internalized racism can be a divisive force, creating a desire in people of color to be white. In addition, the accumulated life experiences of racism can have a lasting effect on one's perceptions and feelings about self and identify.

Developing a Racial Identity

In every person's life, an identity is developed usually somewhere around adolescence. A person's identity gives them a sense of self so that one can answer the question, "Who am I?" The steps to finding any identity include a diffuse state, a foreclosed state, a moratorium state, and an achieved state. One begins in the diffuse state, where there has been little exploration and no psychological commitment to a particular domain. Then a person starts to make a commitment, based on their roles or beliefs, often influenced by their parents and close peers, without the person really considering alternatives. Then when the person reaches the moratorium state they start to explore these beliefs that they never really analyzed or considered before. Lastly, when the person reaches the last state of achievement, they create a state of strong personal commitment to a particular dimension of identity following a period of exploration.

For most white teenagers, they don't often think of their identity as being which racial or ethnic group they are a part of. White people aren't reminded on a daily basis of their whiteness, or the advantages that come along with being white, therefore they never really think of finding their identity in terms of analyzing their race and how it relates to people of color. An example of a model that whites could experience for finding their racial identity. Exploring the racial identity of a white person involves six stages. It begins with the contact stage, where a white person grows up without really thinking there is much racism or discrimination in the American society. They see themselves as the norm and that they aren't racist or prejudice in any way. Most white people never move beyond this stage of thinking.

The next stage is the disintegration stage, where a person experiences an act of racism.

For example, they could witness the police harassing an innocent person of color. The person then begins to notice all of the racism, prejudice, and discrimination going on all around them that they never realized was going on their whole lives. At this point, the person either just shrugs it off or they deal with what they have just encountered. Usually the person will have feelings of hurt, anger and guilt. We all like to think that we deserve the good things we have received, and that others, too, get what they deserve. Social psychologists call this tendency a 'belief in a just world.' Racism directly contradicts such a notion.

After the person has witnessed this racist action and has decided to face reality, they become an anti-racist, which is the re-integration stage. As an anti-racist, the person sees that most whites are racist, whether active or passive, and they find themselves becoming an outcast. Searching for a place to fit in, the person now reaches the pseudo-independent stage. They begin to wish they weren't white because of all the guilt and shame they are facing. So, in order to escape the shame and guilt, they try to become part of the black world or some other world of color. This does not work because people of color cannot relate to what they are going through.

As the person enters the emersion/immersion stage, they begin to realize that they can only relate with other anti-racist whites, who have been through the same thing. They have now found a support system that helps them to unlearn their racist ways and cope with their feelings and emotions. The person now can mix freely with people of other races and see them as individuals and yet still as members of their race. They are still white, but now with a much deeper and more solid understanding of what that means. The person has reached the last and final stage: autonomy. After a white person has completed all the stages of development they are now ready to face the world, doing the best they can to make it a better place for all peoples. Unlike whites, for people of color, their identity usually comes in the form of finding their racial identity.

Racism and Culture

In my opinion black racial identity is defined as the process of exploring one's African culture. Since the early 1970's, there have been numerous theories proposed as to how people come to terms with African culture. Nigrescence is defined as the process of finding ones identity as a Black person. Black racial identity progresses through stages, which range from an individual having no connection with his/her African culture to the same individual gradually gaining an insight and acceptance for his/her own culture.

Nigrescence model includes five stages. The pre-encounter stage is characterized by an individual having views that would be considered anti-black. People in this stage identify more with another race or culture. Extreme ignorance or miseducation of how pertinent race is to ones' sense of self is a possible explanation for pre-encounter beliefs. The encounter stage is characterized by an individual experiencing a situation, whether negative or positive, which in turn forces them to re-evaluate their feelings towards their own race. During this stage, the individual may be faced with psychological distress. In the immersion-emersion stage, an individual superficially immerses him/herself into Black culture and views all other races as negative. The immersion part is characterized by behaviors such as the individual suddenly dressing in African attire and joining groups dedicated exclusively to the African American struggle. During the emersion phase of this stage, the individual begins to evaluate ways in which they were successful (or not) in their quest of becoming comfortable with their Black identity. The internalization stage is characterized by an individual having a deeper understanding and acceptance of his/her Black culture.

An individual may have a "Black Nationalist" identity, meaning he/she has an understanding of what it means to be Black and who he/she is without race being a predominating factor in his/her life. The individual may also take on a "multicultural" identity in which he/she not only accepts his/her own race and culture, the individual also embraces and respects all other identities in regards to religion, social class, gender, and sexual orientation. In the last stage, internalization-commitment, the individual is committed to the striving for the advancement of the African American race. The individual develops a strategy for helping to progress the conditions of other members of his/her racial or cultural group.

Racial salience is the level to which race is the most significant component of the individual's self-concept, which can change in any given circumstance. Racial ideology and regard are comprised of descriptions of what being African American truly is about. In my opinion racial ideology is described as the view in which all African American people should conduct themselves, in accordance with the morals and values of his/her culture.

In my opinion the idea that it is important for African Americans to acquire an awareness of their culture and heritage. It has been proposed that the model of African Self-Consciousness, which is a way of life that African American people should accept. African Americans, as a whole, do have a common way of thinking, feeling, and behaving. There are four fundamental beliefs and behaviors that one needs to acquire in order to have a healthy African Self-Conscious. The first belief includes having a complete discernment of one's Black culture. This includes having a complete respect for everything related to Black culture. The next one is an acknowledgment of what it takes for the African American culture to endure and expand. Therefore, it is important to not only have an understanding of what is important for the success of African American people and culture, but it is also important for African American people to do whatever it takes to continue with the positive growth of the community. The third belief includes having a deep understanding and reverence for all things included in the African culture. Lastly, in order to have a healthy African Self-Conscious, an individual must understand that there is a specific manner in which to deal with others who are not included in the African culture.

The Effects of Black Racial Identity

African Americans face issues concerning their race every day. Racism can be both detrimental to the Black culture and the effects of racism on the individual can be deadly. Racism accounts for many physiological concerns such as hypertension, increased heart rate, and cardiovascular disease. In my opinion that not only can physiological distress result from negative racial identity, but skin color, as it relates to institutionalized experience of racism, can also account for hypertension. I found that darker-skinned African Americans were more at risk than lighter-skinned African Americans for developing hypertension. This can probably be attributed to the fact that darker-skinned African Americans tend to be victims of racism more that lighter-skinned African Americans. A possible reason for this outcome is the fact that lighter-skinned African Americans tend to be thought of as being of mixed race.

I can say that dark-skinned, African Americans are disadvantaged in others arenas compared to lighter skinned counterparts. Many researchers noted that colorism, or treatment of individuals based on the "color" of their skin, has been an increasing trend in literature and it occurs both within and across the African American culture. African Americans were less likely to hold political office, tend to be less educated, of lower socioeconomic status, and are usually given lengthier prison sentences than lighter skinned African Americans.

Internalized Racism and Its Effects

Internalized racism arises when African Americans accept negative racist stereotypes about their own race. Racist stereotypes are based on some of the unacceptable behaviors of African Americans. An example of this would be the stereotype that African Americans are disproportionately unemployed because they are born lazy. The internalization of such racist fallacies can cause individuals to refute their own culture and connect with another. In my opinion internalization of racial beliefs can cause self-alienation in African Americans, causing them to "identify with their oppressor", even to the extent of imitating their oppressors' external appearance.

Some individuals went a step further and introduced the term internalized racialism. I have said in many lectures that not only do African Americans internalize negative stereotypes about their own race, they also internalize positive stereotypes. An example of a positive stereotype that Blacks may endorse is African Americans are better athletes than Whites. I also noted that having a positive view about one's own race can be a positive defense mechanism for psychological distress. There is little empirical evidence on the effects of internalized racism on an individual's psychological and physiological health. However, the effects of internalized racism are detrimental to the mental and physical wellbeing of an individual. Internalized racism has been linked to mental health issues such as depression, self-alienation, low self-esteem, and aggression.

EDUCATIONAL IMPACT OF RACISM ON BLACK CHILDREN

Black Racial Identity and Academics

In my opinion physiological areas, racial identity also plays a role in other areas, such as academics. I have a perception that the Academic achievement of gifted African American students who tend to receive poorer grades in school and African American males tend to exhibit more negative racial identities, such as preen counter attitude, than those who are academically successful. Many attributed this to the fact that males and underachievers may lack motivation to succeed academically in part because they fear what their peers may think of them. It is possible that they do not want their cohorts to believe they are acting like the White students, who are perceived as overachievers. So, to further separate themselves from the white overachieving students, they may not work to their full potential.

In my opinion racial identity can affect one's academic success and self-esteem. Many researchers have found that racial consciousness plays a key role in identifying academic self-efficacy, specifically in African American males. Many have also noted that in order to effectively educate African American students, the educator should first identify what stage of racial consciousness the students are in. For example, a student who is in the encounter stage may have more anger towards the white race due to the racist situations they have faced.

Achieving Success at School and "Playing White"

Black students in high school today learned quickly that they must navigate between the dominant white student group, the non-dominant Black student group and home. The experience was similar to learning another language. Students talked about playing white when they referred to themselves trying to achieve academically. Playing white referred to a means of surviving in the mainstream, whereby students must speak and write Standard English, as opposed to their native colloquial speech. However, some of their Black peers criticized this behaviour; they felt that those students playing white were pretending to be better than they were, and in the process ignored their Black peers.

Even outside of class's students must observe a whole series of cultural symbols, social customs, language usage, dress and body language, for example ways of walking. Students understood that there was a price to pay for playing white: See, like there's people just don't hang with their own color, because I don't. A lot of people consider me as a preppie: It's the way you talk, the way you carry yourself. We have college prep classes, get respectable grades. The groups I hang with we don't yell out loud and run down the halls. Students such as this one understood the second-class status that has been assigned to their community and try to disassociate themselves from this status, at least at school. These students believed that schooling would help them achieve their career goals and ensure both a college education and gainful employment. Such students must suffer being ignored by other less academically invested Black students.

This playing white phenomenon seemed to be a recurring theme in the stories of those students whose goal was academic achievement. Other elements contributed to the success of students in high school: the presence of teacher role models; good principals and vice-principals; strong support for each student in the school; the ethnic makeup of the community in which the school was located; and high standards and expectations required of the students by the teachers at the school. First, the presence of teachers who were good role models gave students a message: the role model has gone through the system, has survived, and has come back as an example of what was possible. The role models made achievement seem normal, not unique, and certainly within reach. As well, principals and vice-principals, in addition to being good role models, steered the school in a particular direction depending on how they interpreted and implemented rules and policies. Second, strong support for each student was an important element of an effective school. In a school with strong support, each student should be able to find his/her own place in the school and should be able to develop a sense of belonging. In addition, if the school was in a multi-ethnic community, which was both welcoming and supportive, students' self-confidence would reach higher levels. All these factors and more were necessary to make students succeed.

I have gone through a study which focused on twenty teacher candidates of color, found that these teachers were committed to becoming teachers because of their lack of role models as younger students. It can be said that few role models existed for these individuals as beacons of hope or success in a dominant white society. I have a perception that work documents how Black female teachers assume the role of mothering' their students. Black students experienced racism in school, but fortunately there were other forces working against institutional racism. These forces and positive policies allowed students to feel that they belonged in the school, that they were persons first, and that the color of their skin was not a major factor affecting their success. Administrators at the school were often Black, meaning that proactive decision making could occur at high levels within the school. Also, strong affirmative action policies were in place, prompting school administrators to examine school policy and its impact on all students. Together, these elements within the school helped students to feel that they belonged, that they were persons first, and that the color of their skin was not a major factor affecting their academic success. This notion of playing white was a reality for Black students as the above. However, my work concurred with the avenues for students not to have to play white. If the atmosphere in the school was such that Black student achievement was required, expected and demanded, then peer pressure could be reduced to the point where it supported achievement.

Resistance

Of the many students who hoped for and applied for U.S. athletic scholarships only one or two percent were able to realize this dream. These athletes and other Black students should be working towards their high school diplomas, but in reality spent their time in high school gyms perfecting their athletic skills. These students often were the victims of low teacher expectation in academics and thus the stereotype of the "Black athlete". Perhaps Black working class children would not reject or resist schooling if they could see the following:

a)   that their parents' hard work was rewarding;

b)   that they could get a job for which they are qualified;

c)   that their school environment reflected them and was inclusive; and

d)   that their teachers had standards which they were expected to meet.

For this to occur would involve large societal changes which extend beyond the sphere of the school. Some Black youth gave up on education and its promises and have instead linked their hopes for a better future on the slim chances of an athletic scholarship.

Blacks in the curriculum, provide academic support programs, introduce anti-racist education, ask teachers to recognize the uniqueness of each student, hire more Black teachers and coaches and have coaches provide more support and guidance. Many immigrant parents sacrificed for their children because they wanted their children's lives to be better than theirs. This first generation succeeded in school. The second generation children of Black immigrants were the ones who looked at their parents and saw that they did not do that well that the education and hard work still landed them in dead-end jobs or left them unemployed or under-employed. They saw that their parents experienced racism. This generation was the one, who often resisted the institutional system. Some resisted in small ways, while others rejected the system entirely.

The small things students did to resist include, for example, coming habitually late to school, cutting classes, or hanging in the halls, (which resulted in suspensions and time off school). All of these actions hindered their academic progress. Black cultural norms in U.S. schools and discovered when students found they were in conflict with the curriculum, students' effort for schoolwork declined. When I looked at student conflict with the curriculum, they were referring to the relevance the curriculum had in their lives. What was the connection between the students and the curriculum? When students realized that they were getting a 'second best' education they rejected it. Similarly, in British schools, what happened in school was a representation of what was happening to the Black community socially and economically in British society. They concluded that the ways that students resisted education in schools should be seen in the wider context of the racial discrimination against the whole Black community in British society. There were similarities in the researchers' work that led me to develop the framework of the student interviews.

This discrimination experienced by Black youth and the Black community was different from the racial discrimination experienced by Asian youth. Asian students were stereotyped into perfect academic students, which was sometimes an unattainable objective for some students. On the other hand, as has just been discussed, Black students were stereotyped as being poor at academics and good at sports. Both groups were being stereotyped and were subject to racism.

I argued in Unraveling the "Model Minority" Stereotype that the idea of a model minority was a denial of racism and structures of racial dominance and that it silenced those Asians who were not economically successful. In addition, this stereotype also served to silence the racial injustices experienced by African Americans. That is, the stereotype seemed to imply that: 'if we can make it on our own why are you not able to?'. The Model Minority stereotype supported the status quo and the ideologies of meritocracy and individualism. It was used to prove that social mobility was possible if you just worked hard. It placed the burden of failure on the individual and not on the system. It pitted groups against each other. It placed Asian Americans and African American in adversarial positions.

The contrasting stereotypes confronting these two minority groups work on the distinct realities of different minorities. Many claimed that, in the North American context, there were two kinds of minorities: voluntary and involuntary. Voluntary minorities were those who chose to come to the U.S. for a better life. Involuntary minorities were those who had no choice-they came to the U.S. either through slavery, like African Americans, or through conquest, like Native peoples that voluntary minorities did well because they saw schooling as a step upward in social mobility. All the discrimination they faced culturally and linguistically was simply a speed bump on the road to success. Involuntary minorities, however, have rejected the dream that success in school will lead to future success. Because of persistent social and economic discrimination, involuntary minorities did not believe in economic success or social mobility. The involuntary minorities underachieved in school because they viewed schooling as a threat to their oppositional cultures and identities.

I also observed that immigrants and children saw the second generation as non-achievers. However, important comparison into a group's perception of schooling and that group's achievement in school, I saw Asian students as a monolithic group with shared achievement levels and shared attitudes towards schooling.

RACISM AND ITS AFFECT ON SELF ESTEEM, SELF-CONCEPT, AND SELF IDENTITY

Racial identity

I can defined the racial identity as a collective conscious, as group identification, and as a two-dimensional construct. In my opinion racial identity as a process by which an individual recognizes his or her racial group as a salient racial group. Similarly, racial identity as self-identification with a particular ethnic label, based on the perception of belonging to an ethnic group. It can also be said that racial identity as coming in contact with, or becoming familiar with, members of one's stereotyped racial group.

Racial identity serves as a tool through which African American males can effectively confront the overt and covert discrimination and prejudice they face on a daily basis. Racial identity has been linked with important psychological and social factors that influence the development of African Americans. It is an important tool African Americans use to combat the negative social influences they encounter on a daily basis. In addition, several models of how racial identity develops have been proposed that provide the foundation for counselors to help African American males achieve a positive sense of racial identity.

In my opinion African American's identity development as a duality of consciousness in which one strives to be American without experiencing missed opportunities because of the color of one's skin. The process of racial identity is a dynamic maturation process and involves a series of distinct and discrete stages. Individuals move from identification with the dominant culture and rejection of one's own culture to a heightened level of self-concept and comfort with one's identity. In my opinion racial identity development as reflected by the changes and consistencies of one's self-image and used expansion of ego identity development as the driving force. I believed that African Americans are in a constant state of fluctuation and changes in self-images and that they never truly achieve their own sense of self. In my opinion racial identity development as shifts in one's worldview or consciousness and believed that these shifts occurred in sequential stages. Many have sought to expand on previous models of racial identity development by incorporating the intersection of social diversity and social justice with an individual's level of personal beliefs, attitudes, and behaviors.

In summary, racial identity has been identified as an important tool for the effective education of African Americans in educational settings and in society. The understanding and connection to one's salient reference group is an important component in the life course development of African Americans. In addition, the importance of racial identity in the development of a positive sense of self-worth and self-esteem among ethnic populations.

Self-esteem

In my opinion self-esteem is congruent between one's ideal self and real self. Similarly, self-esteem as a set of attitudes and feelings that an individual has about herself or himself. Self-esteem is one of the most widely held concepts in the psychological sciences and some counseling theories rely on self-esteem as a significant explanatory variable of positive mental health, development, and holistic well-being or wellness. I have identified self-esteem as an important component in helping African American men construct realities that promote social status, social mobility, and occupational prestige. It is a central mental health component that shapes the development of African American males from adolescence to and throughout adulthood.

Because of the increased participation by African American males in higher education, have begun to evaluate the effect self-esteem has on their academic achievement. For example, the importance of self-esteem in both African American male college students and African American professionals. The impact of social alienation on the self-esteem of African American males on predominantly white college campuses. Students who displayed high levels of self-esteem and a positive self-image were more likely to have lower levels of social alienation. They also were more likely to return to college for another semester. In my opinion self-esteem is an important component for the social development of African American males. Because of the strain society places on the African American male population, it is difficult for them to feel good about their identity. Positive self-esteem has been dearly established as a vital component in the development of the African American male and as an important tool in helping them to cope with social pressures and racial discrimination. As a consequence, a variety of programs have been developed for the African American male population designed to increase their self-esteem and self worth. These programs include Afrocentric rites of passage programs and education or school-based programs designed specifically for African American males.

In my opinion all these approaches have had positive effects on some delinquent and educationally-impoverished African American males who have not received the services they need from traditional educational and social programs. The common assumption that delinquency exists in every African American male limits the applicability and success of many of these programs. Though these programs have been effective in increasing self-esteem in some of the members of this population, they continue to view the problems of African American males from an illness perspective and are reactive rather than proactive. A strengths-based program offers a more comprehensive approach and may provide the critical components necessary to address the complex self-esteem needs of the African American male population.

Programs to Enhance Self-Esteem of African American Males

The lifespan impact of self-esteem on African American males has been well documented, as have correlates of positive self-esteem. These correlates provide a foundation for the development of programs to enhance self-esteem, especially in young African American males. These programs include Afrocentric rites of passage programs and education or school-based programs designed specifically for African American males. These approaches have had positive effects on some delinquent and educationally-impoverished African American males who have not received the services they needed from traditional educational and social programs.

Afrocentric rites of passage

An example of an Afrocentric rites of passage program that focused on African American males in the juvenile justice system. The in-home therapy approach is based on the African principle of naturalism and creates an optimum environment for building a therapeutic relationship. The family is given the opportunity to define who constitutes the family, and sessions are scheduled once a week. The sessions are designed to enhance effective parental discipline, positive self-concept and self-esteem, happiness, family cooperation, and emotional strength. Individual sessions are scheduled for the African American male adolescent in the home and focus on developing his strengths, capabilities, attitudes, and self-esteem through incorporation of the principles of collectivity and spirituality. The interventions emphasize the interplay of community support for the individual and the individual's support of the community. Counseling continues until the adolescent demonstrates attitudinal and behavioral lifestyle changes.

After-school group counseling. The Rites of Passage program includes an afterschool adolescent group in which African American males work together to make lifestyle changes by fostering new relationships and building positive self-esteem through the personal and cultural strengths of the group. Family Enhancement and Empowerment sessions require that parents attend monthly parent training seminars and semiannual family therapy retreats. These are educational treatment interventions that help families to develop cohesiveness, support networks, and strong parent-child relationships. African American males learn to develop more effective problem-solving skills and to make appropriate decisions necessary to manage their behavior, especially in both community and school settings.

Education programs

While the Rites of Passage program focuses on African American males in the juvenile justice system, other programs have been designed to address the needs of African American males in educational settings. The establishment of African American male immersion schools designed to address specific problems of African American male students who are educationally at risk. These schools distinguish themselves from traditional schools in that they provide a curriculum for African American male students that are distinct and different. The curriculum is designed to address the unique needs of African American males and is designed to increase self-pride and self-esteem.

Characteristics of immersion schools. Immersion schools have seven distinct characteristics that distinguish them from traditional approaches:

(a) a male mentoring program,
(b) the incorporation of "Rites of Passage" activities,
(c) the provision of tutorial assistance,
(d) the implementation of an Africentric curriculum in addition to the prescribed curriculum,
(e) the incorporation of a "families" concept,
(f) a strong emphasis on student management and family intervention, and
(g) special requirements for teachers assigned to the school.

The schools have implemented different activities designed to develop intellectual achievement, self-awareness, self-respect, and self-esteem. This approach has been implemented in urban school districts across the United States.

The immersion schools may be more effective in fostering students' personal responsibility for their academic achievement. They recommend that continual comparisons be made between immersion and traditional programs to address the effectiveness of immersion programs in addressing self-esteem in adolescent African American males. They also recommend a longer time frame for effective implementation of the program. Initial analysis shows no significant differences on self-esteem levels between immersion and traditional third-grade students, but there is a need to be completed to gather empirical data that speaks more directly about these schools and their impact on the self-esteem of African American males. The need to cultivate young African American scholars is not limited to entire schools but has also been addressed through specific school programs.

School-based programs

Project P.R.O.M.I.S.E. is an elementary school reading and mentoring program in many urban communities in the United States designed to address the problem of academic achievement, search for identity, and role identification for African American boys. This school-based program focuses on developing appropriate male role models, increasing academic skills and values, strengthening the parent/community connection, and increasing identity and self-esteem. The intervention strategies are designed to address the basic competency skills that typical successful students have developed: academic and survival skills, positive self-concept and self-esteem, communication and interpersonal skills, coping ability, and control over decisions, behavior and their future.

Component parts of project P R O M I S E. The component parts of project PROMISE include intensive staff development, peer mediation, after-school tutorials, parent-community relationships, and field trips to a historically Black university campus. Students are selected according to academic need and willingness to participate. Mentors receive training geared towards meeting the special academic and social needs of the students and work with the students at least four times per month, providing tutoring and mentoring services. The students accompany their mentors to university campuses to help them experience the world of education that is available to them.

Evaluation is an ongoing process and involves each participant. While it is an informal approach, literature supports the notion that mentoring programs of this type can be more effective than professionally trained counselors alone. Students and parents that participated in these programs report an increase in their children's vocabulary, willingness to learn, self-concept, and academic achievement. The program provides a positive framework through which African American males can operate, which helps to promote increased identity and self-esteem.

In summary, developed programs for the African American male population designed to increase their self-esteem and self-worth. Though these programs have been effective in increasing self-esteem in some of the members of this population, the weakness of these programs is that they view the problem from an illness perspective and are reactive rather than proactive. Because they assume, erroneously, that delinquency exists in every African American male, these programs can only be applied to a limited number of African American males in the total population. A strengths-based program offers a more comprehensive approach in addressing the needs of the African American male population.

RACISM AND ITS IMPACT ON THE HEALTH OF BLACK CHILDREN

Relationship between Black Racial Identity, Internalized Racism, and Depression

I have a perception that socioeconomic status, education, marital status, and employment have been link with depression. Likewise, ethnic differences in relation to depressive symptoms. African American children have higher rates of depression than White children due to living situations with parents, lack of support, and being more likely to have a debilitating medical issues.

With the first proposal of the Racial Identity Attitude Scale, that psychological distress was linked to negative racial identity attitudes (pre-encounter and immersion-emersion). Some of the noted stressors were anxiety, low self-esteem, aggression and hostility, and inferiority. The psychological effects of racial identity, the effects that racial identity has on African-American's psychological functioning. Black college students, indicated that individuals in the pre-encounter stage of racial identity were more likely to show signs of psychological distress such as anxiety, memory impairment, paranoia, hallucinations, and alcohol abuse.

African Americans may develop "invisibility" syndrome in which they begin to devalue their race and self-worth. This lack of self consciousness can ultimately cause African Americans to harbor damaging stereotypes about their own race. There is a connection between increased levels of depression and internalized racism. A positive correlation between increased levels of internalized racism and depression. Black, single mothers in Pittsburgh, Pennsylvania, there was a significant association between high scores on the Beck Depression Inventory and high scores on the Racist section of the Nadanolitization Scale.

The correlation between Black racial identity and internalized racism. Perceiving that there may be a connection between the two, the impact that racial identity and internalized racist stereotypes have on one another. The sample population included 153 Black college students. It was found that there was a positive correlation between individuals who associated with a race other than their own and high levels of internalized racism.

Social and Emotional Health Impact on Children's Development

A new goal for Healthy People 2020 is focusing on early and middle childhood. One area this goal aims to analyze and improve is social/emotional health. Young children's socio-emotional health is important to their development and success later in life. This success has the potential to enhance education attainment, future employment opportunities, and contributions to society. The connection between racism and discrimination and its impact on children's social/emotional health as exhibited in their respective Head Start environment. The current body of literature by informing environmental and biological outcomes of children's social/emotional health including social responsibility and premature births; more specifically, on how race-related events influence the various dimensions of risk factors associated with these stressors. Parent's experiences with racism and discrimination and its effect on young children's social/emotional health outcomes is a growing body of literature.

Racism as a Stressor

The concept of racism as a specific type of stressor common to people of Color in the United States has been advanced over the last decade by a number of scholars, and is informed by the social and racial cultural critique of transactional models of stress and coping. Three related models of racism (or discrimination and prejudice) as a stressor, which are grounded in the evidence of the relationship between racism and mental and physical health outcomes, have emerged in the literature.

With respect to stress as a psychological experience, the ways in which prejudice and discrimination might impact the primary and secondary appraisals of events as stressful. Additionally, certain characteristics that are common to discriminatory events (attribution of the event to internal, stable, and global causes), and which have been correlated with negative outcomes, may lead to the appraisal of increased negativity and therefore greater stress. Furthermore, socio-cultural aspects of oppressed group membership (e.g., access to tangible resources, availability of social support) may influence the secondary appraisal of coping, which could result in a decreased sense of coping efficacy and increased negative impact of the stressful event.

For example, hostile expressions of anger have been linked to greater cardiovascular reactivity. In addition, socio cultural norms and expectations associated with oppressed group membership may influence the types of reactions people have to stressful experiences. For example, particular aspects of a common experience such as schooling may be perceived as more stressful for Blacks than for Whites as a function of the experience of racial disparities and differences in mainstream socialization messages about race and education. I have found that socio-cultural factors may influence the selection of particular coping methods, which may in turn attenuate or exacerbate the stress response.

Since racism and racial discrimination have become increasingly subtle and covert over time, objective reports of discrimination can be difficult to ascertain. Although use of this model has generally predominated in the literature and there has been widespread acceptance of the role of cognitive appraisal (i.e., subjective perceptions) in generic stress (i.e., general non-racial stressors), some scholars continue to question the utility of relying exclusively on subjective measures of discrimination in the mental health consequences of race-related stress.

The links between racism and health outcomes, failed to utilize an empirically testable model. Therefore, many have proposed a biopsychosocial model of racism as a stressor for African Americans, which hypothesized specific relationships and potential moderators and mediators. It has been argued that when an environmental stimulus is appraised as racist it leads to exaggerated psychological and physiological stress responses, which may account for some of the health disparities that are consistently reported between Blacks and Whites. It has been pointed out that individual responses to racism are influenced by constitutional, socio demographic, psychological and behavioral factors, as well as coping responses which may serve to moderate the impact of race-related stressors. Constitutional factors may include skin color, family history of hypertension, income, and occupational status. Socio demographic factors include socioeconomic status, and psychological and behavioral factors include personality characteristics, self-esteem, and anger expression suppression.

These factors may also interact with one another to influence the relationship between racism and psychological and physiological outcomes. Thus, different levels of exposure to race-related stress as well as differences in coping strategies may account for within-group variability in health and mental health outcomes for African Americans. The importance of subjective appraisal (whether or not an incident is perceived to be racist) as central to the resulting outcomes, and argue that different coping responses (active vs. passive, general vs. race-specific) may have an impact on the types of outcomes people experience. The immediate psychological and physiological reactions to race-related stress will likely influence peoples' selection of particular coping responses.

There are a number of antecedent variables (e.g., race/ethnicity, gender, age, socioeconomic status, sociopolitical and geographical contexts), which may have an impact on the frequency and intensity of particular types race-related stressors people experience. Cultural values, acculturation status, and worldview on perceptions of discrimination and as mediators of the relationship between racism and outcomes should be considered. Thus, the introduction of the concept of racism as a stressor brought a greater deal of specificity and the impact of racism and discrimination on mental health. In addition, the development of the concept of racism as a stressor has been accompanied by the creation of a number of scales to assess the frequency and impact of experiences of discrimination and race-related stress. These measures have advanced the concept of racism as a stressor by providing more reliable multidimensional means of measuring discrimination and race related stress than the single-item measures used in earlier investigations.

The measures of race-related stress have been used in psychology examining the relationship between racism and various outcomes, which has provided further evidence for the conceptualization of racism as a stressor.

POVERTY, CRIME, AND DELINQUENCY, ITS IMPACT ON BLACK CHILDREN

Poverty and Crime

I have a perception that academics and policy practitioners have long acknowledged the unquestionable yet complex relationship between poverty and crime. Poverty stricken areas are more susceptible to crime. Moreover, poverty has been shown to have a disproportional effect in some locations while engendering social transformation throughout the larger metropolitan area of which it belongs. Cities continue to face a dilemma in which extremely impoverished neighborhoods routinely become breeding grounds for high rates of crime. This picture of persistent crime concentrated within a select number of poor neighborhoods has been a mainstay in criminological literature and remains influential in the development of policies aimed at addressing poverty and crime related issues. Recently, however, a new proposition has emerged arguing that as poverty becomes less concentrated and more widespread or dispersed throughout a city, additional social problems such as higher rates of crime can ensue. Based on these assertions, my objective is to determine the extent to which changes in the composition and distribution of poverty impacts neighborhoods and the overall level of city crime.

Historically, cities across the U.S. have undergone changes with respect to how poor populations are geographically situated. During the 1970s and 1980s, poverty populations became overwhelmingly concentrated. This led to a significant growth in the number of extremely disadvantaged neighborhoods (poverty rate greater than 40 percent) throughout America's largest cities. An outgrowth of this configuration was an increase in the number of social ailments found within these areas. During the 1990s noticeable changes occurred in the geographic distribution of poverty. In other locations, however, the number of high poverty neighborhoods began to decline accompanied by an increase in the number of neighborhoods with more moderate levels of poverty. The efforts to address problems associated with poverty accompanied by a major push to redistribute poor populations could be one reason for these changes. Another possibility is that natural forces of ecological change were responsible for this reconfiguration as some locales experienced gains and losses of individuals from various socio-economic backgrounds. Nonetheless, the overall implications of the compositional changes cities have undergone have yet to be determined.

Past attempts to explain city crime rates have shown that cities that differ in key physical and structural characteristics have varying levels of crime. Besides providing a basic understanding of the correlates of crime, these characteristics provide further evidence as to why crime flourishes in some locations, but not in others. City crime rates has focused primarily on city level characteristics, the theoretical explanations used to explain variations in city crime rates implicitly apply to conditions found at the lower geographic levels of analysis such as the neighborhood. The amount of crime that a city experiences, is in part a product of the city's compositional features. These features are an aggregation of the city's neighborhoods and other components that are representations of the larger ecological landscape.

Understanding the process of urban change occurring throughout these smaller parts of the larger ecological environment has enabled us to investigate transformations taking place throughout the city as a whole. For example, the human ecology model partitioned the city of Chicago into zones undergoing changes that differed in terms of physical, economic, and social characteristics. It was believed that the ills of society such as crime, poverty, illiteracy, mental illness, and alcoholism were linked to the inner-city core areas. In my opinion crime persisted in poorer minority neighborhoods due to the transitions occurring within these zones. Hence, deconstructing the city into separate parts has been and remains a common approach to explore processes operating within cities and the role of neighborhood contexts as explanations of crime.

Neighborhood characteristics such as poverty have received substantial attention interested in explaining the emergence and persistence of social problems such as crime. The process by which neighborhoods are negatively affected by these features depends in part on the scale and overall distribution of these characteristics. Furthermore, documenting the role and evolution of these underlying neighborhood characteristics remains a critical element when attempting to understand and explain differences in crime within and across cities. Several competing explanations have been offered describing the extent to which underlying structural conditions of neighborhoods are conducive to crime. On specific measures such as the poverty rate to represent the context of a neighborhood. A different approach and use a composite measure of concentrated disadvantage that combines several dimensions of a neighborhood.

Whether the formal definition of poverty or a concentrated score of disadvantage is used, both approaches imply that communities that are resource deficient have a higher likelihood of crime. Regardless of the methodological construct, the poverty status of a neighborhood is one element that each definition has in common. Poverty is one of the primary components needed to classify a neighborhood as extremely disadvantaged when using a composite measure of concentrated disadvantage. Moreover, additional factors such as high unemployment, female headed households, and residential instability are commonly found in neighborhoods with high levels of poverty. Because of the similarities between the constructs of poverty and concentrated disadvantage, these terms are commonly used interchangeably. Therefore, both approaches underscore the structural inequities that are tied to the poverty status of neighborhoods and cities. As neighborhoods become more impoverished, a number of demographic changes arise that affect the stability and structure of neighborhoods. The growing problems and social dislocations that emerged as a result of the demographic transitions occurring within inner-city neighborhoods. Neighborhoods that experienced economic and social decline eventually became comprised of a disadvantaged underclass population.

The environmental and contextual features embodied within these neighborhoods can create conditions and situations resulting in a higher likelihood of crime. In fact, some of the highest rates of crime are often found to be concentrated within areas suffering from economic hardship. In my opinion violent crime in the city of Chicago varied significantly depending on the economic status of the community with the highest rates of violence found in communities of underclass status. Poor neighborhoods have higher rates of violent crime. Thus, levels of neighborhood poverty may signify one of the most common underlying elements in areas with high rates of violent crime. A link between violent crime and poverty have fostered the notion that more crime is an unavoidable consequence of community decline. This logic has also been applied to explain the effects of poverty on levels of property crime. The general rationale implies that as levels of poverty increase, crimes will also rise.

Juvenile Delinquency and Juvenile Crime

Delinquency is behavior by a minor that is antisocial or in violation of the law. Status offenses are activities that are deemed offenses when committed by juveniles, because of their age at the time of the activity. Some offense would include not attending school, breaking curfew laws, running away from home, and possession and consumption of alcohol.

The comparison of juvenile courts and adult courts are: The juvenile courts are adjudicated in a civil proceeding, juveniles will have no criminal record, and have the ability to get record expunged and sealed once the juvenile reaches adult hood. In the adult court adults are charged in a criminal proceeding and upon a finding of guilt carry a criminal record for the remainder of one's adult life. One difference is juvenile courts are conducted in an informal manner, focus more on Paren's Patria versus Due Process, court records-recordings of proceedings is the decision of the juvenile judge and the preponderance of the evidence used in most circumstance other than determine delinquency, where beyond a reasonable doubt is implemented.

Now adult courts proceedings are very formal, are courts of record, and the standard of proof required to determine a guilty verdict is beyond a reasonable doubt. Only 39 states have no guaranteeing juveniles the Right to a trial by jury. Defendant in adult court has the Constitutional Right-safe guard to have his or her case determined by a member of one's peers- Jury trial or a bench trial. In juvenile courts juvenile judges are limited when imposing punishment to juvenile and will either issue one of three dispositions: nominal, dispositional, or custodial.

There are many variables that cause juvenile delinquency. Sometimes juveniles want to test their parent's limits, or society limits. Some people believe that imposing strict laws such as curfews will causes drop in juvenile delinquency rates but sometimes imposing strict rules give juveniles more of an incentive to break the laws. Also lack of rules and supervision could cause juvenile crimes to occur. An example would be most kids commit crimes after school or when their parents are at work or preoccupied. In some case mental illness and substance abuse can be contributing factors to juvenile crime rates. About 20% of juveniles have mental illness, and 30-90% of convicted juveniles when the scope of mental illness widens. Some say juvenile crime rates can be due from divorced, or a child with one parent.

Many believe a child environment and family are greatly related to their juvenile delinquency record. Poverty level is another factor that is related to chances a child has of becoming a juvenile delinquent. Relationship a child develops in school or out of school can be a factor. A positive or negative friendship can have a great influence on a child chances on becoming delinquents. Peer pressure can come into play, along with gangs contribute to violent crimes of delinquents. Statistics show that there are roughly 75 million juveniles in the United States. That is one in four Americans have the potential of being labeled as juvenile delinquents.

Juvenile crime rate dropped for two consecutive years. Negative changes in the economy can affect all crime rates due to people are more likely to find themselves in pressing situation like unemployment. Changes in population can affect juvenile delinquency rates. Also social changes, such as educational or health reforms, could have a large impact on juvenile crime rates if they create a large population of at risk children.

The effects of juvenile being tried as adults are: Juvenile offenders will receive sentences in the adult criminal system which is harsher and more proportional to their crimes. Some chance that if a juvenile is tried as an adult in criminal court may actually result in higher rates of reoffending. Juvenile also can received longer sentencing. Issues in the juvenile justice system are Mental Health services. The lack of the services makes it hard to treat the juveniles with these disorders. This includes a lack of community based services for juveniles' offenders who are not in detention. The juvenile system also lack sufficient addicting and substance abuse treatment resources. Education is an issue in the juvenile system also. With all of these issues how can we expect juveniles to stop committing crimes and being delinquent if we do not create the resources for self-improvement.

One has to make funds available for improving the programs that needs the most focus. Educational programs would be a start because most juveniles are school drop outs. Improving this would help. Also improving the mental health programs or resources will probably stop the continued detention of juveniles that do not need to be in detention centers.

The Importance of Delinquency Prevention

Many children pass through these systems. They first enter the child welfare system often proceeding into the mental health care system, then into the juvenile justice system and finally into the adult correctional system. This common progression of "at risk" children through child and youth services and into adult institutional systems illustrates the inability of these social services systems to achieve their mandate either separately or in cooperation with each other. The pain and suffering that results from the failure of these social services is felt not only by these young children passing through these systems. These children become parents and often pass on their disadvantaged circumstances to their children and so on through generations. The theme of this thesis asserts that criminological aspects has substantiated that a number of specific childhood risk factors correlate to later juvenile delinquency. The second theme of this thesis contends that criminological aspects have found that several programs, which address these risk factors, can substantially reduce the likelihood of future delinquency.

Third, criminological aspects concludes that the criminal justice system has proven to be somewhat ineffective at reducing crime, in part it does little to address the risk factors that correlate to criminal behavior. The criminal justice system, by its very nature, can only respond after a crime has been committed and can do little to prevent crime. Fourth, the implementation of preschool intervention is discussed. Several programs which focus on reducing these early risk factors are outlined and synthesized in this thesis. These programs include: the Perry Preschool Project, the Yale Child Welfare Project, the Houston Parent-Child Development Centre, the Syracuse University Family Development Program, Better Beginnings, Better Futures Project, and the University of Rochester Nurse Home Visitation Program. These programs are important in that they illustrate repeatedly through evaluations that certain components of these programs can effectively address early risk factors and reduce later criminality.

To reduce delinquency," it is important that we take action by using proven methods of intervention that will reduce criminal behavior. When discussing the importance of preventing crime and making communities safer, it is crucial that we not lose sight of the balance between how successful the approach is, and what the total economic and human cost of the intervention is for society. Efforts to reduce crime must respect the dignity and quality of human life for the victim, the offender and society.

RACISM AND ITS IMPACT ON THE ACADEMIC PERFORMANCE OF BLACK CHILDREN IN AMERICA

The educational system in the United States has historically failed in attempts to achieve parity in academic outcomes across racial and socioeconomic groups. While the magnitude of academic disparities decreased with the elimination of overt discriminatory practices in the educational system, differences in achievement between Black and White students persist within schools and are evident in student outcomes. Current statistics demonstrate that racial disparities between African-American and White students in K-12 education are present in all areas of the schooling experience, including performance on standardized tests of reading and math achievement, participation in special education and gifted programs, rates of discipline, graduation/dropout rates, and college attendance rates.

According to the National Assessment of Educational Progress, approximately 14% of Black students and 45% of Whites, reached basic grade-level competence on 4th grade standardized measures of reading and mathematics, leaving more than 85% of African-American students and 55% of White students performing below basic grade-level competency. Statistics worsen as students increase in age, with approximately 10% of African-American students and 38% of White students are meeting basic levels of reading and mathematics competency according to eighth grade standards.

African-American students are also overrepresented in special education programs and are disproportionately subject to disciplinary proceedings. While African-American students represent only 17% of the student population nationwide, they account for over one-third of all suspensions and are twice as likely to be designated at mentally retarded or emotionally disturbed. Additionally, African-American students have significantly lower high school completion rates than their White counterparts, where only approximately 50% of African-American students graduate from high school as compared to the 75% completion rate for White students. These disparities significantly impact the percentage of African-American students that go on to attend four-year colleges and those who are able to find sustained employment. There are also significant societal costs and consequences, where a high school dropout earns on average $10,000 less per year than a high school graduate and $28,236 less per year than a college graduate.

In my opinion educational outcomes are also associated with involvement in the criminal justice system, where the overwhelming majority (68%) of inmates in state and federal prison have not earned a high school diploma. Thus, poor educational attainment outcomes significantly limit the life chances and future opportunities for African-American students. Though racial disparities in education have been widely acknowledged, move beyond critiques of individual student ability, motivation, and family non-participation to analyze the educational structures and practices which affect African-American students and maintain racial disparities in educational attainment.

In my opinion, there are several policies (e.g., the allocation of federal and state resources; teacher qualification, distribution, and compensation), and practices (e.g., ability tracking, unequal disciplinary practices, cultural incongruence, teacher expectations) associated with persistent racial disparities in achievement. While these policies and practices reveal distinct racial disparities that have disproportionately negative consequences for African-American students, educational policies and practices are typically not discussed as manifestations of institutional or individual racism.

The elements of racism and discrimination are present on societal, educational, and individual levels and are detrimental to the academic performance of African-American students. The literature suggests that societal inequality, negative racial stereotypes, and negative interpersonal interactions affect the ways in which African-American students perceive and interact with schooling institutions, resulting in decreased academic identification, academic performance, and engagement with the educational process. It is limited in its exclusion of analyses of the effect of within-school practices (e.g., discipline, curriculum) and racial disparities in educational policies (e.g., resources, teacher distribution) on the academic outcomes of African-American students. In examining the achievement outcomes of African-American students, are limited by their exclusion of the other. Thus, conceptualizing educational policies, practices, and interpersonal interactions that negatively and disproportionately affect African-American students as manifestations of institutional and individual racism allows for a comprehensive analysis of African-American students' schooling experiences, perceptions of racial injustice and discrimination, and associated achievement outcomes.

Conceptualizing Racism in Schooling Institutions

In my opinion racism is a system of dominance, power, and privilege based on racial group designations, occurring where dominant group members create or maintain structures, ideologies, values or behaviors that have the intent or effect of leaving non-dominant group members excluded from power, esteem, status, and/or equal access to societal resources. Within this definition, racism has also been conceptualized as a multidimensional construct, which includes institutional, individual, and internalized manifestations of racism. Institutionalized racism refers to the differential access to goods, services, and opportunities in society by race, while individual racism refers to differential actions of prejudice and discrimination based on race enacted by individuals. Internalized racism reflects the acceptance by members of stigmatized racial groups of the negative messages about their value, ability, and character. In the educational context, the analysis of each dimension of racism is critical to understanding the presence of racism and student experiences with racism within schools.

The conceptualization of racism as endemic and pervasive in the lives of African-Americans is also discussed within Critical Race Theory (CRT), providing a theoretical lens to address the achievement disparities affecting African-American students. Critical Race Theory emphasizes the role of institutional racism in explaining the sustained inequity that people of color experience in educational settings through manifestations of racism in the curriculum, instruction, assessment, and school funding. Given the definition of racism and the critical race theoretical approach to understanding racial disparities in educational outcomes, this current investigation conceptualizes racism as manifested in educational settings through institutional structures and educational policies, school practices, and interpersonal interactions within the school context.

Racism in the educational policies and structures of schools is present in school culture and curriculum, disparate school funding, resources, and facilities, teacher qualification and distribution. Racism in school practices is observed in ability tracking and disciplinary practices. Individual racism in interpersonal interactions within the school environment can be observed in discriminatory behaviors and prejudiced attitudes between students and teacher interactions, treatment, and expectations of students of color.

Due to the multiplicity of manifestations of racism within schooling institutions, it is imperative to examine the manner in which African-American students experience and is impacted by racism within educational contexts. In my opinion description of racism as experienced through direct, vicarious, and trans-generational mechanisms, it follows that, interpersonal racial discrimination and African-American student outcomes must be expanded to also include student perceptions of structural and school inequalities that disadvantage the individual, members of their racial/ethnic group, and/or affect the larger racial/ethnic group over time. It is hypothesized that the experiences of attending a poorly-funded school, witnessing or experiencing vast disparities in discipline practices, and/or being racially victimized by a classmate or teacher can all have consequences for African-American students' interpretation of equity and racial justice in the schooling process and may ultimately affect academic motivation, engagement, and achievement.

Racism and African-American Students: Implications of Racism in School Contexts

African-American adolescents' experiences with racism and analyzed the impact of racism on the academic achievement of African-American students. In the societal context, African-American adolescents report experiencing mistreatment in their community, daily hassles or micro aggressions in public settings, and a generalized awareness of racism in society. Within schools, African-American students perceive racism in teacher-student interactions, disciplinary actions, peer interactions, and school practices.

Student perceptions of racism in larger educational policies and structures maintaining racial disparities, such as funding policies, resource disparities, and academic tracking. Additionally, a single element of racism within the school context, such as teacher-student or peer interactions, a comprehensive analysis of racism (e.g., including educational policies, practices, and interpersonal interactions in school settings) has not yet been conducted. This current investigation examine the depth and range of African-American student perceptions of racism across the school context, specifically analyzing perceived racism in educational policies, school and classroom practices, and interpersonal interactions.

It is provided significant evidence suggesting that perceived racism has overwhelmingly negative effects on the educational outcomes of African-American students. African-American college students demonstrate that perceptions of racial stereotypes can negatively affect the test performance and academic identification of high-functioning students in stereotype threat situations. In many experimental situations, African-American students performed less well and dis-identified with tasks in conditions where they feared confirming negative racial stereotypes. The presence of intellectual stereotypes and activation of stereotype threat has also been linked to psychological disengagement, devaluing, and discounting feedback in the academic domain. The psychological mechanisms associated with experiencing racism and discrimination within academic settings, which have implications for academic performance, academic self-concept, and identification with the schooling process.

Perceptions and experiences with racism have also been linked to increased distrust, expectations of negative treatment, and development of an oppositional identity in educational settings. Similarly, experiences with racism in schools and in larger society have been associated with academic disengagement and poor academic outcomes among students of color. African-American adolescent societal discrimination experiences were negatively related to academic engagement, academic curiosity, persistence, and grades, and positively associated with an increase in problem behaviors at school.

SOCIAL ISSUES AFFECTING BLACK CHILDREN

Social Competence Issues Regarding Black Children

A review of the social competence literature would not be complete without mention of special issues regarding Black children. The social competence of ethnic children should be informed by all additional factors effecting that development due to ethnic group membership. However, have mostly emphasized the negative consequences of group membership that deviates from mainstream culture. The positive effects of the Black community and culture on the social development of Black children will also be discussed. In my opinion competency skills and the development of competence varies according to culture. Different competency skills develop that are relevant to the child's ecological and cultural circumstances. Thus the repertoire of social competence behaviors for Black children may include different skills than the repertoire of behaviors for other ethnic and cultural groups.

In my opinion Black child development in the context of the extended Black family. I had discovered how the extended family influences child development and family life. Child development needs to also consider the positive impact of the Black community and culture on childhood development. The negative consequences, deficits and deficiencies of Black child development. Black children are genetically, intellectually inferior or socially and cognitively handicapped, crippled and damaged due to racism and poverty.

It is argued that the deprived environment of Black children seriously damages their mental health, psychological well-being. For instance, discuss the relationship between social policy and the mental health of Black children. Many report that Blacks in urban areas, with economic related stress, and cut backs in federal spending and social programs for the poor place individuals at risk for emotional, social and cognitive developmental problems. The oppression and racism detrimentally damages Black children's self-esteem. Neglecting to consider the Black cultural context has led to the failure to consider coping responses and adaptive reactions to stress and racism for Black individuals. It is profoundly wrong to assume that Black people have been overwhelmed by the destructive influences of the racist society. It is one thing to recognize the social handicaps that impede the fulfillment of an individual's potential. It is quite another thing to conclude that the handicap has crippled him.

The Deficit Model has been the predominant framework used to explain how racism, poverty and oppression affect children and adults. Specifically how families cope with the stress and strain of racism in their lives. A stress and coping model for Black families. The basis for their model is that Black families have developed coping strategies to combat and confront mundane extreme environmental stress. A similar model of the factors that build and potentially threaten the self-esteem of Black children is needed. Black children and individuals possess high levels of self-esteem. A number of factors are mentioned as responsible for the reported high levels of self-esteem.

A racial insulation and attitude of significant others as important factors for the self-esteem of Black children. High self-esteem of Black children can be attributed to being raised in the Black community and attending Black schools. In my opinion immersion in the Black community leads to high self-esteem of Black children. For neglecting participation of Black fathers in childhood development. Many researchers state that father-child interaction patterns are related to positive self-esteem of Black children. Although racism, oppression, poverty and socio-economic stress may threaten Black children's self-esteem, some literature suggests that stress and trauma stimulates the development of coping behaviors. I present three reactions to threat to self-esteem. First, an individual may be overwhelmed. Second, an appropriate response may be elicited or third, a mixture of healthy and unhealthy responses may emerge. The range of appropriate responses includes anger or "Black rage" and "cultural paranoia".

Black behavioral responses to racism and their mental health consequences. The response types included continued apathy, seeking a piece of the action, obsession with counterculture alternatives, the Black nationalistic alternative, identification with an authoritarian solution and cognitive flexibility through awareness of Black history.

It appears that healthy and adaptive reactions to socio-political-economic stress and threats to self-esteem are important and relevant social competence skills, especially for Black children. After all, social competence includes, an individual's everyday effectiveness in dealing with his environment. As these specific skills are relevant for Black children's social competence, other groups may possess other culturally specific competency skills. The entire set of social competence behaviors, including the culturally specific competence skills will enable the child to manage his own ecological and cultural environment.

Parenting and Black Families

The concept of contemporary parenting has begun to focus on and examine how culture and race interface with the relationship between parenting and child socio-emotional development. Culture appears to play a major role in the way children are reared and in their development. However, the community possesses little knowledge of the relationship between parenting and child development within different cultural and ethnic groups.

An ecological model of the predictors of parenting behavior to assess teen-age parenting skill. The predictive factors included punitiveness, knowledge of developmental milestones, depression, personal social support, age and race. Many researchers reported that age, race and punitiveness significantly predicted the score on the parenting skills measure. Older white mothers with less punitive attitudes scored the highest on the parenting skills measure. It is confirm that generally parents of higher SES and Caucasian parents tend to be more permissive in there parenting style, while Black mothers and low income mothers tend to be more restrictive.

The age of mother was related to parenting and may be related to infant mental development. Younger Black mothers evidenced much less optimal parenting than older Black mothers. Older Black mothers were more likely to design a supportive home learning environment, were more responsive, less punitive and more able to support the intellectual development of their infants. Programmatic and intervention efforts should prove to be more valid and reliable, which reconfirm the differences between ethnic groups. An ironic trend in the literature shows that early intervention training programs teach mothers to be less restrictive, punitive, and more verbal. The trend of intervention programs however, appears to value the parenting styles of high SES parents and Caucasian parents, despite the contradictory results and conclusions regarding restrictiveness and firm control.

Low SES and Black parents may differ in parenting practices from the mainstream for positive and adaptive reasons. In my opinion SES differences in childrearing may reflect adaptive adjustment to social environmental conditions. The different parenting practices of Black parents reflect a cultural adaption approach. I propose that Black families adapt to values controlling the child's public behavior more than white families. It is necessary for the professional community to carefully evaluate the programmatic and treatment efforts with Black families and parenting practices. In my opinion very little is known with regard to intervention effects on family processes and how cultural background impacts that relationship.

SUICIDE AND BLACK CHILDREN

In America, one suicide is completed every 17 minutes. This unique act is a non-discriminatory method of death, as it impacts individuals from all walks of life. Although rates among groups differ, suicide affects individuals of various age, sex, socioeconomic status, race, and educational levels (among other factors). In order to understand the totality of suicide, it may be beneficial to examine it in detail among groups. One group of particular interest in recent years has been young African American males. Historically, African Americans have completed suicide at much lower rates than Americans of European descent. However, there have been significant changes in suicidal patterns among African Americans, namely an increase in the rate of suicide completion and nonfatal suicidal behavior among adolescent and young adult African American males between the ages of 15 and 24. From 1980 through 1995, the suicide rate among young people increased by 146% for African American males.

The highest number and rate of suicide within African Americans is found within the adolescent and young adult population. For African American youth age 15-24, suicide is the third leading cause of death behind homicide and unintentional injury. For purposes of this review, risk factors associated with suicide among young African American males will be explored. The term risk factor will be used to describe any factor that is associated with an increased likelihood in suicide or suicidal behavior. It is important to note that risk factors do not necessarily imply causation.

Notion of Suicide

The notion that suicide and homicide are different manifestations of the same causal process is articulated as the "stream analogy," sometimes called the "stream of violence theory". Stream analogy suggests that various social forces, economic and status deprivation, in particular, generate impulses toward violence that can be expressed inwardly or outwardly, depending on whether individuals can identify an external source at which to attribute their circumstances. Those who can identify an external oppressor have a tendency to express outward violence, usually in the form of homicide, and those who cannot identify an external oppressor will attribute causality for their circumstances to themselves. This is theorized to create a tendency toward suicide.

The stream of violence argument is often used to account for differences in homicide and suicide rates among those in various social groups. For example, the lower suicide rates among Blacks in the U.S. compared to whites is often explained by the stream analogy. Because Blacks may attribute causality for their economic deprivation to dominant whites, they will, presumably, express violent impulses outward in the form of homicide. A partial test of the stream of violence theory that focuses on variations in suicide among Blacks and whites in U.S counties. For centuries, suicide and homicide have been considered, respectively, as murder of the self and murder of another.

The main foundation for the suicide and it has advanced a tradition by which suicide and homicide as distinct phenomena. The conditions that create an imbalance in social integration and social regulation.

Moreover, suicide and homicide can be mutually exclusive, respond similarly under the same conditions, and respond differently under the same conditions. Suicide and homicide can coexist and this was particularly the case for anomic suicide and homicide. Anomic suicide was theorized to stem from a decrease in social regulation, but a decrease in social regulation was not found to explain homicide. Therefore, suicide and homicide may not be generated by the same causal factors and many findings seemed to refute the assumption of stream analogy that suicide and homicide are different manifestations of the same causal conditions. In my opinion suicide and homicide can simultaneously increase under the same conditions . Such observations rejuvenated stream analogy as scholars tried to explain potential exceptions to the typical inverse suicide-homicide relationship.

Racial Image

Before black individuals entered the United States their image had already been constructed by white men. These stereotypes had a detrimental impact on black individuals as they have been faced with exaggerated images that have depicted them as inhumane and sexually lewd individuals. Contemporarily, the media has helped perpetuate negative stereotypes on African Americans living in the United States. The images and pictorial stereotypes are seen in the past, as well as contemporary movies, TV shows and commercials, news broadcasts, comedy shows, music, etc. These negative depictions and portrayals of blacks have formed a racist society which still remains today. One would think that today, a century after the unjust era of slavery in our democracy, the stereotypical and racist images of African Americans would be extinguished. Instead, racism still exists in our societies and does so with strong and negative effects. Historical conditions of the past, including slavery and segregation, have shaped society as we view it today. Stereotypes of the past have streamed into today's modern images and pictorial stereotypes. Today, one can see how mainstream media resorts back to old stereotypes. The many myths and ideologies of the past have remained with us and have been passed down generation after generation with the help of media.

For instance, images of African Americans began with the Jezebel stereotype and that stereotype still continues today. The media perpetuates African Americans in negative connotations divided in dichotomous categories; they are either asexual or sexual. Other images include blacks as criminals, violent, and aggressive. These images, however, dispute reality yet have constituted, took over, and controlled the cognition of past and present generations. I will discuss African American stereotypes of the past and connect them to those of the present. I will discuss how ideologies of the past were meant to justify the negative treatment of African Americans which resulted in the expanding of stereotypes in media and their acceptance in society.

The portrayal of race has been constructed through media and has been a mere process of selection. This process of selection is one which can be seen throughout history that has come to build this idea of white supremacy and justification of inequality. The representation of others as inferior serves as a purpose in justifying the negative treatment of others and keeping whiteness as the ideal. Not only do these pictorial stereotypes serve as a justification of unjust acts, they serve to construct and ensure white supremacy through the oppression and exploitation of others. Past as well as contemporary representations all trace back to the myths that were created to justify the inhumane conditions of the past, especially that of enslaving African Americans. Of course, after hundreds of years of being fed spoonfuls of this negative stereotypes and hatred, it eventually gets internalized and has a psychological impact on

African Americans giving them a sense that they are hated and inferior which leads to feelings of anger and frustration.

Black individuals were brought to the United States for labor in the 17th century. Upon arriving in the United States, their identity was already constructed by white men who traveled to Africa. These Europeans were astonished to find women who were polygamist and semi-naked, when compared to the white puritan women. At that point, the constructions of the monolithic categories of black individuals were created. Whiteness remained and was a result of the oppression of others. Individuals who associate themselves with groups that are being negatively depicted have internalized the stereotypes and are being fed inferiority, hatred, and frustration in a nation "built upon the exploitation of people of color to ensure white supremacy." The racialization and construction of different groups in different ways justified their treatment and status in society.

Some of the more famous images of the past include: the Mammy and Sambo. These portrayals of African Americans were brought about to justify slavery and to send out the messages that African Americans were actually happy slaves, which I would consider to be an oxymoron. Mammies are depictions of African American women with exaggerated features. African American women were portrayed as unattractive and asexual Mammies. The Mammy is always brought about as an overweight female, with a big smile to show her 'happiness' as a slave, whom is obedient to her master. Other features include big lips, a gap in between the teeth, bulging eyes, dark skin, etc.

The Mammie caricature helped serve white America both socially and economically. The Mammie, depicted as happy and obedient to her master as a house servant, was meant to serve as a form of justification in solving the moral dilemma of slavery. It also served as a way to boost the economy as it was used in advertising household goods such as baking powder, pancake mix, coffee, etc. One of the more famous Mammies is Aunt Jemima, who is still seen today on the shelves of many stores. The image of Aunt Jemima was first portrayed by slave Nancy Green over a century ago. Today, the image of Aunt Jemima is much different than past images as "she now has the appearance of an attractive maid." Aunt Jemima is just one of the many stereotypical images of the past that still exist in today's society. This image is one example of how past images exist in modern forms. These images and messages have been in our society for a great period of time and continue to grow as part of our society, sending the same messages of the past into the present and future.

The image of Sambo, was used to send out a much different message. The Sambo expressed blacks as childlike and irresponsible. It is complicated to imagine an individual happy as a slave, yet this was depicted in many different forms. An image of blacks with an exaggerated smile is one way this idea of happy slaves was expressed. This cultural image of the Sambo was meant to fantasize happy blacks in happy places in order to resolve the moral conflict of allowing slavery in a free and democratic society. It sent out the message that African Americans were not normal, were inferior, and different from everyone else. Yet these images were found appealing to society, which leads to the assumption that they were of some value to the people.

As slavery came to an end, the extreme caricatures began to fade away in the 1960s. However, an end to one aspect of pictorial images of stereotypes did not put an end to the continuous cycle of racism. Segregation led to new images of black individuals. Due to segregated public facilities, African American youth found nowhere to turn to for recreational activities; as such activities like boy scouts were for the white kids only. As a result, African American youth began forming clubs as a source of recreation, acceptance, power, and competition. Police and society however, began labeling these clubs as threatening and violent gangs. Police brutality emerged to maintain order as an effect of this prejudice. These negative labels were internalized and as a result of police brutality against blacks, chaos emerged. The newly formed clubs rebelled against society as a way in bringing self worth upon themselves. They wanted to prove to others that they were not inferior by spreading feelings of pride and power within themselves. With this rebellion came even more violent acts of police brutality leading to violent mass protests and riots that came to construct these new stereotypes of blacks as the face of crime. A new era rose within the media, it created a new image of black individuals which put an emphasis on the violence and brutality of blacks. These new images had the same psychological impact on blacks, giving blacks a feeling of worthlessness, hate, frustration, and anger that they have come to internalize.

It also brings about the division of the black community into binary categories which are the old generation and the new generation. The old generation grew up internalizing the images of the Mammy and Sambo, which was viewed as faithful. Meanwhile, this new generation of blacks was looked at to be rebellious, violent, and aggressive. The image of a black man resisting arrest or being brutally and forcefully arrested by the white policeman is an image that is heavily repeated in media. These new images, similar to the old images were portrayed through different streams of media including, but not limited to television shows and commercials, news broadcasts, movies, comedy shows, and music.

When looking at television shows, commercials, and news broadcasts, one can easily see how the African American race is depicted. TV has come to shape the American culture. The imagery brought out through TV has come to govern our cognition, behavior, and conception of life. The constant repetition of the stereotypical images on TV has come to define society. The bifurcated images of not only race, but also of gender, have constructed social expectations, roles, and rules of socialization. Media's strict division of the black community has come to define this racial group in two: the wealthy vs. the poor. Media's split images are opposite of reality yet are heavily depicted. This paragraph needs something.

Again, in the 1960s, the extreme caricatures started to fade, meanwhile the depiction of violent acts by blacks started to rise. Media reports on stories of race in very particular ways, especially through news broadcasts. In cases where the suspect is of color or of a minority group, the media has had and continues to have the power to generalize an entire group based on this one individual. When acts of violence are committed by a person of color, the media comes to generalize the entire group rather than report the story as an exceptional crime. However, in cases where the suspect is white, the media comes to categorize it as an unusual or extreme incident. Despite documented cases like that of white female teachers having sexual relations with underage males of color, the issue of race here is ignored. Meanwhile, in cases when a white female accuses a black male of rape, the stories receive extreme exposure through media. Provide proof Stories in which the victim is a person of color are more likely to be ignored, while those of white victims are emphasized with the assumption that the crime was committed by a person of color. These particular ways in reporting stories on race have cultivated fear in one race; praise in another.

The exploitation of blacks can be traced back hundreds of years ago during the slavery era. Over a century ago the defining of African Americans as inferior was an effect of the many branches of the justification of racism. The exporting of African Americans from their homeland into a land where they would face enslavement was just the beginning. One cannot put enough emphasis on how unjust the era of slavery was, yet there were many ideologies that arose in hope to justify this act. One of which was depicting African Americans as chattel which came to produce about more images of blacks as jezebels, bucks, and breeder women. After emancipation, the image of the black rapists emerged. This image was a result of southern whites' fear of blacks' promiscuity as a threat to the southern way of life. Again, the idea of keeping white supremacy and womanhood formed this new myth of blacks as rapists and criminals; which as a result is still seen in today's modern society.

The many ideologies of blacks as savages, inferior, aggressive, threatening, etc. have all been expressed through the media. The negative images were meant to serve as a purpose in keeping blacks separate as they were labeled as an inferior and different race, lying in the middle of the spectrum as the link between humans and apes. Not only did the pictorial images of blacks project them as inferior and violent, but also as sexually promiscuous. Stereotypes of black sexuality developed through images in media that came to define gender expectations and roles.

The exploitation of black femininity was resulted through the depiction of black females' hyper sexuality. Black females are sexually exploited through images that depict them as sexually promiscuous. Black female sexuality was constructed into popular songs and this type of sexuality was suggested as sexual service for money, power, and pleasure. Black women were depicted as sexual property and the myth that it was impossible to rape a black woman because they were already promiscuous helped mask the sexual exploitation of black women by their owners. This ideology of black promiscuity in females was yet another form of evidence to justify racism. The racist notion that blacks were closer to animals than any other human race was another approach in exploiting one race in hope to praise white supremacy. The inhumane act of dehumanizing one race had a psychological effect on blacks in which they came to internalize the stereotypes. Furthermore, this act of dehumanizing was accepted by society and with this acceptance we can see why it continues to flourish into our daily lifestyle and culture.

As a result of the depiction of black female sexuality the development of the concept of the "bitch" versus the "freak" arose, which again was just another way in trying to justify these negative stereotypes. The term freak was used to express sexual deviance, sexuality outside the normal boundaries, and proximity close to animals while the term bitch was divided in two: the "Bitch" and the "bitch." The capitalization of the B in Bitch came to express an admired, strong, and tough female, while a "bitch" with a small "b" was the negative evaluation of the female. These depictions served as forms in exploiting women yet have transformed into aspects of our daily social lives. These negative perceptions are expressed heavily in hip-hop and R&B music, comedy shows, etc.

In contemporary hip-hop and R&B music the terms bitch and freak are heavily used and have come to transform modern societal vocabulary. These terms have been used an overwhelming amount of times in modern music and media that we have almost come to take away from their negativity. Media's redundancy of these images has resulted in society's generalization of many ethnic groups. Minority groups are faced by these negative portrayals of themselves in media; these images get internalized as a result of the constant repetition. Why these depictions are still portrayed in a nation that strives for equality? The answer lies in the past. After hundreds of years of negative portrayals and oppression of minority groups, the concept transformed into a part of media. Representations in today's societies are based on past ideologies that were created to justify the unjust conditions of the past. Although the many negative contents of the past have faded, they still exist, but they do so in new forms.

Today, media continues to have special ways in reporting stories on race. However, many members of the audience tend to ignore these depictions as they have grown into our daily lifestyles due to their constant repetition in media. Media's effect on society has come to negatively generalize one racial group as inferior with little power and low status in society. With that said, can we conclude that news media is credible? I believe in some cases we can, in others we must be careful as we can most definitely come to conclude that media deals with the issues of race through selection. The images of race are not completely ignored as the audience continues to realize racial differences in reports, yet with the constant repetition of the portrayals they are most definitely losing value. It is not surprising in today's society to hear stories of a black male suspect on the lookout or any person of color. What is surprising is that these depictions are completely accepted by society. Very few come to question why one race is always associated with the same act and generalized by doing so. We simply come to accept it. The lack of analysis and critical thinking of this aspect results in the proliferation of these pictorial stereotypes and waves of racism that have been spread throughout the nation. It is a concept that if ignored will only continue to spread rapidly, having the same psychological affects that it has had in the past and continues to have today. It is simply a continuing cycle of cause and effect that has yet to be broken. Historical conditions of the past have everlasting effects on the present and will continue to do so for the future.

Constructing race is a collective process and practice which produces a distinctive set of meanings. As a society we have constructed race. We began to categorize by race as a form of shorthand within the community: gender, race, religion, etc. We have come to associate both negative and positive ideas to the concept. The many symbols of race that I have outlined, including but not limited to skin color, language, origin, mannerisms, facial features, clothing (whether it be associated with religion or pop culture), class, etc., are what we look for to define or interpret race. We read these symbols and use them to construct stereotypes of others, and with the help of media these stereotypes spread like wildfire. They convey negative feelings to those who are being categorized; feelings of alienation, hostility, and worthlessness to name a few. Race is an illusion that we created and has been with us since the beginning of time. This illusion of race has led to the loss and/or denial of humanity to those of non-white ethnic groups. Because race was created so long ago and continues to live with us as a part of our society, it is hard to imagine a world without this illusion.

Race is unavoidable. Media strengthens this statement with its pictorial images and stereotypes of race that have transformed our societies. This idea is seen everywhere, it is most heavily seen in the American society because of the many diverse cultures that make up the American culture. With that said, we can conclude that media is extremely powerful. Its depiction of race has come to form stereotypes that have had negative effects on society. 100 year old stereotypes still exist today in their new forms and are expressed through the different streams of media that have transformed today's society. Race is a concept that was created by society's illusions yet is has developed, transformed, and influenced our culture and continues to do so. We can come to the conclusion that history truly does repeat itself, and we can expect that our futures will hold the same racist notions that were held today, yesterday, and a century ago. It is a never ending cycle; unfortunate yet unavoidable.

Renewed Interest in the Stream of Violence

The connection between suicide and homicide, it clearly did not completely stifle such debate about the issue. The variations in suicide rates relative to homicide rates among low status and high status groups. It drew on the Freudian concept of frustration-aggression, arguing that unemployment generates aggregate levels of frustration. In my opinion, suicide and homicide are inversely related and that both respond to frustration, as measured by unemployment rates. The consistently higher suicide rate of high status groups was explained as due to a weakened relational system and freedom from external regulation.

Family dissolution was taken to indicate weakened involvement in social relations, as well as from external restraints. This freedom was said to increase the legitimacy and tendency towards internal attribution of causality and suicide. The consistently higher homicide rates among low status groups were interpreted to result from a strong relational system and external constraints over behavior. This lack of freedom from societal constraints requires lower status persons to conform to the demands and expectations of others. Therefore, those in subordinate positions, or in intense social relationships, have less control over their own actions and circumstances. This lack of control makes it less difficult to attribute causality for frustrations to others because circumstances are perceived to be outside of one's control.

For instance, many proposed that it is socialization toward aggression rather than the strength of the relational system that explains the direction of lethal violence. It has been contended that patterns of socialization determine whether aggression is manifested inwardly or outwardly, despite societal constraints. Higher status individuals do not necessarily have fewer external constraints on aggressive behavior than do individuals of lower social status. Lower class parents, on the other hand, were more likely to spank or threaten to spank their children. As a result, children from lower class backgrounds are socialized to possess an "action tendency" (aggression) towards others. This "action tendency" is a potential explanation of why those with lower class standing have a greater propensity for homicide than suicide. Internal attribution is considered as attributing causality for circumstances to oneself while those who engage in external attribution attribute causality to external sources. Instead, homicide was found to be positively related to income inequality while suicide was positively, but curvilinearly, related to economic development. Thus, it provides only partial support for the stream of violence interpretation. Further, a regional effect was found in the higher homicide rate for the South. This was interpreted as a result of cultural, structural, and historical factors that arguably make external aggression more acceptable in the South and increase external attribution by southerners.

In my opinion, as a test of the frustration-aggression hypothesis despite omitting unemployment rate and divorce rate as indicators. By omitting these key variables in favor of economic development and income inequality, the analysis allegedly becomes a test of the attribution thesis rather than a test of the frustration-aggression hypothesis. The measured components of frustration-aggression and attribution using: income inequality, economic development, divorce rates, and unemployment rates.

For stream of violence to control structural forces of production as well as both structural and cultural forces of direction. In U.S. counties, measured structural inequality and deprivation as forces of production, and immigration and racial segregation as forces of direction. Partial support was found for the stream analogy. Infant mortality, a measure of deprivation, was the most significant force of production, but with regard to the direction of lethal violence, racial antagonism was shown to have only a weak effect on the tendency of suicide over homicide. I also studied on county-level bivariate and multivariate analyses to test three explanations for the relationship between social deprivation and lethal violence. The first, the attribution hypothesis, explains that internal and external attributions of causality shape the direction and target of aggression and lethal violence. The second; the socialization hypothesis addresses environments that suppress outward expressions of frustration. The third explanation is the social disorder hypothesis, which proposes that social disorders such as unemployment and family dissolution increase both suicide and homicide, thereby creating a positive suicide-homicide relationship under those specific conditions.

The percentage of immigrants, racial residential segregation, and relative deprivation as measures of likely attribution. Higher percentages of immigrants, relative deprivation, and racial residential segregation were considered to be indications of resource competition and inequality. Percentage of college educated residents and the percentage of professional workers were taken as measures of socialization. Social disorder was measured using the divorce rate and percentage of female headed households. Bivariate analyses revealed a positive relationship between suicide and homicide. However, the multivariate analysis showed an inverse suicide-homicide relationship, and there were higher homicide rates but lower suicide rates in counties with higher immigration, relative deprivation, and racial residential segregation. Therefore, findings were interpreted as support for the attribution hypothesis in which suicide supposedly increases with internal attribution of causality for socioeconomic conditions whereas homicide increases with the availability of external sources at which to attribute causality.

The findings of early and more recent stream of violence highlight some inconsistencies in the factors that produce and direct lethal violence among general populations and among status groups. There is greater consensus regarding the role of economic conditions as forces that produce the total amount of lethal violence, but less agreement has been reached concerning which factors direct lethal violence to take the form of either suicide or homicide.

There has been a rise in suicide rates among Blacks, particularly manifested in younger generations. In my opinion, younger generations of Blacks are more exposed than their predecessors to environments that foster poor mental and emotional health, and that these younger Blacks lack the protective factors that were available to older generations of Blacks.

There may also be a generational shift toward greater internal locus of control, as younger generations of Blacks come to perceive that their own efforts and investments dictate the outcomes in their lives. Hence, if the stream of violence theory is correct, documented increases in suicide among younger generations of Blacks result from an increase in the general status of Blacks. Most recent generations of Blacks should be more likely to direct violent impulses inward in response to what are perceived as individual failures.

In review, the stream of violence argument proposes that if Blacks can be shown to have gained in status in a particular context or period of time, their suicide rates should have increased also. On the other hand, if Black status has demonstrably declined under various conditions, then their suicide rates should have correspondingly decreased. Finally, when Black suicide rates rise or fall, scholars can look for evidence of a corresponding rise or fall in status markers. For example, if the violent impulses generated by deprivation produce more suicides among lower status groups and if suicide among Blacks increases, one should also observe an increase in educational and occupational attainment and prestige among the general Black population. But, it is needed to address some unanswered questions regarding the economic indicators that generate violent impulses as well as the status markers that direct violent impulses for Blacks and whites.

ELIMINATING RACISM AND ITS IMPACT ON BLACK CHILDREN

New conceptualizations of racial attitudes

In my opinion, a recent attempt to consolidate social psychological and counseling theory on white racial identity, the three underlying dimensions of racial identity. The first is obliviousness vs. awareness of social inequities based on race. The second dimension is stereotype-based vs. experiential knowledge of non-whites, while the third dimension is whether the burden of accommodation to ameliorate racial injustice should be on blacks or on whites. Ordering these dimensions into four clusters, the first cluster includes unawareness of racial inequities, stereotyped knowledge of blacks, and placing the burden for change on blacks to fit into white culture.

The gap between theory and measures

Several of the psychometric problems in scales relate to the inclusion of more than one construct per scale. The lesson to take from this problem is the importance of creating discrete scales. Being aware versus unaware of unfair black disadvantage is a separate dimension from being aware versus unaware of unfair white privilege. Awareness of black disadvantage suggests sensitivity to the dilemmas our culture creates for those who are not white.

In my opinion, good psychological health requires a positive acceptance of one's race, there are few questions to assess this acceptance on any existing scales. These ideas can be assessed in three dimensions: whites' unawareness of race in general and inability to see race as a self-descriptive attribute, contact status; whites' awareness of the benefits of being white, related to immersion/emersion status; and whites' pride in their own race.

Dimension 1: Awareness of race Whites' awareness of race in general is theoretically related to the contact stage of avoidant cluster, and first cluster. Yet this dimension does not seem to be assessed by the contact scale, which focuses on curiosity and naivete. Whites' awareness of race addresses a realization that to be white is to have a race, that there are differences among blacks and whites, and that blacks and whites has different experiences in American culture.

Dimension 2: White benefits another aspect of white's awareness of their race is acknowledging the benefits of being white. Being aware of white privilege means acknowledging one's participation in the institutional benefits of belonging to American culture, which is designed to maintain advantages for whites. In my opinion, whites have a sense of entitlement to feel superior to blacks as a basic norm of white society. As the dominant culture, whites can choose whether to acknowledge this entitlement.

Dimension 3: White Pride Whites' pride in their own race is parallel to measures of black pride. In the Black Racial Identity Attitude Scale there are a number of items addressing positive feelings about being black ("I believe that being Black is a positive experience," "I feel excitement and joy in Black surroundings," "I believe that everything

Black is good, and consequently I limit myself to Black activities," "I believe that because I am Black I have many strengths").

Dimension 4: Identification with blacks A dimension addressed in theory but not in measures is the identification with black's attitude is reactive type. This type as identified more strongly with blacks than with whites, idealizing black culture. This is a form of racism, since it describes differential responses to blacks and whites based on race. However, it is a more socially acceptable form of racism that may align with some of the modem or aversive racism constructs.

Dimension 5: Patronizing Another dimension related to the reactive type would be the patronizing white dimension. This includes white people who believe they have directly comparable experiences to blacks in American culture, disregarding the impact of race. This dimension describes one who fits into third cluster as aware of race differences, relying on some experiential and some stereotyped knowledge of blacks, and seeing it as a white responsibility to help blacks fit into white culture.

Dimension 6: Social Responsibility A final dimension is the sense of social responsibility to change the status quo. It also responds to idea that there are different attitudes toward the burden of responsibility for change, and there are economic reasons for whites to maintain a racist culture.

CONCLUSIONS ON
BLACK CHILDREN

Overall, it can be said that racism is still rampant in the lives of African Americans. Given the reality and the stressful nature of this social disease, it is imperative that efforts continue to expose and validate the virulent impact racism has on psychological and physical health outcomes. Such endeavors could further lead to understanding the etiology of stress-related diseases and social problems in the Black community, hopefully with the prospects of offering policy implications. That is, policies that would hold the dominant perpetrators responsible and accountable. In the meantime, it is also important that endeavors continue to unearth combative approaches that would buffer the toxic nature of racism. It suggest that leaning more on a spiritual orientation continue to serve as a source of resiliency in Black people. Finally, this must be extended beyond the walls of academia into the broader community.

The racism and stress associated with the dismantling of affirmative action explain a significant amount of the variance for collective self-esteem and psychological well-being among students of color. So we can say that continuous social change needs to be still made since the rates of unemployment among blacks compared to whites is relatively the same as it was in the early 1960s. Employment opportunities are still hard to obtain for black men while neighborhood segregation is still present in many areas in the United States.

Institutionalization

Fear designed to elicit submissive behavioral responses works best when expectations of negative consequences are high. Expectations of negative consequences are increased when the practices that produce the fears are institutionalized. Institutionalization is the process of establishing an enduring practice, relationship, or organization in a society or culture; a system of procedures or patterns. As per my understanding, internalization refers to culture becoming a part of the self, institutionalization is a parallel process of culture becoming a part of the institutional order, i.e., defining roles, statuses, norms, and goals. Institutionalism originates in the operation of established and valued procedures by respected forces in society through the use of laws, rules, and regulations. Internalized racism is acquired by its intergenerational transmission; through the exposure to institutionalized racial phenomena; and through racialized social institutions.

Racialized fears and the conditioned behavioral responses that are internalized are used to reaffirm institutionalized racist ideas, beliefs, and processes. Institutionalized racist ideas, beliefs, and processes at the same time enhance the racialized fears and the internalization of racism. The relationship between fear and institutionalization operating as a closed positive system perpetuates and maintain each other to continuously reproduce the desired effects of institutionalized and internalized racism. There are a myriad of institutionalized events, laws, rules, and regulations that through social institutions have entrenched fears, values, beliefs, norms, attitudes and behaviors into American culture and onto the psyche of the American people that foster the conceptualization of race that perpetuates racist thoughts, beliefs, and behavior, which are internalized to some degree by all segments of society.

The institutionalization of racism has also had the effect of defining roles for the oppressed and for the oppressors, that when these roles are internalized, predisposed responses reinforces the respective roles and in effect reinforces the internalized as well as the institutionalized racism. This functions as another closed positive system. The learning and the socialization of these roles have also been institutionalized and internalized within family structures and passed down from generation to generation. Due to the organic nature of intergenerational transmission of racist dogma and racism, the constructs of race and racism become deeply embedded because they are passed on as a part of the belief system of each succeeding generation. When racism gets institutionalized in social institutions, it becomes self-perpetuating within institutions and reaffirmed by those who inhabit these institutions because of the learned implicit and explicit information and instructions passed on by the institutions themselves.

The expression of people's attitudes, beliefs and behavior are a reflection of the degree of racist dogma they learned and internalized from intergenerational transmission of racism and from their association with social institutions, with both serving as reinforcements of the racist dogma. These closed positive systems help to maintain institutionalized racism within family structures as well as within social institutions. The insidious relationship between fear, institutionalization and internalization of racism poses a serious challenge for all who live in this society. Fear and the institutionalization of racism are entwined, especially when it comes to the question of internalized racism. Fear helps to promote institutionalization processes for racialized oppression that is internalized; and institutions provides fear with a structure from which it can perpetuate its internalizing effects.

I believed that fear and institutionalization work together to coerce individuals and groups of individuals to internalize ideas, thoughts, philosophy, actions, behavior, beliefs, asserted truths, and lies about racial hierarchy. When the conditioned acquired fears derive strong credence because of the institutionalized basis of negative consequences, it becomes that much easier for African Americans to accept racist stereotypes and capitulate to the established norms. When self-deprecation, self-effacement, abnegation, and the denigration of the Black/African self, culture and beauty are practiced by individuals, the effect is internalized racism. The quintessential threads of fear and institutionalization have woven the race and racism design into the fabric of the American cloth, a design that has always posed a threat to unravel this society.

The institutionalization of racism, and the internalization of racism in an historical evolutionary context. It has afforded us the opportunity to assess the circumstances by which these phenomena have come into existence and how one leads to the other. The devastating impact the activities associated with race and racism have inflicted upon African Americans. This historical context has given us a glimpse of the distorted, complex, complicated and convoluted reality that has emerged from the ruins of a people's culture that have seen them lose their land, family, traditions, beliefs, moral standards, identity, religions, and direction. It is mind-boggling to imagine that for a period of 400 years African Americans have been displaced, murdered, raped, dehumanized, denigrated, mutilated, lynched, burned, experimented on, sacrificed, and defiled.

Fear, institutional and the intergenerational transmission of racism have promoted the internalizing of racism that helped to create attitudes and behaviors that show indications of low self-esteem, self-denigration, self-deprecation, self-effacement, abnegation, with a collective persona that is liberally drenched in self-hatred, which results in the physical, psychological, mental, and spiritual destruction of the African personality. Africans/African Americans have been placed faced-down as the doormat of the world and cast as its permanent underclass, only to have the question asked. What's wrong with them? When asking what is wrong with African Americans, a person, no matter who they are, must be able to within their mind encompass and try to comprehend all that African Americans have encountered and absorbed over the past 400 years, and then place those occurrences in a context so that their perspective can somewhat accurately assess the damage that has been done to African Americans. Just one of the things that are wrong with African Americans is the disproportionate overrepresentation of African American young men's involvement in violence as perpetrators and victims.

Risk Factors for Youth Violence

Risk factors for youth violence are indicators that increase the likelihood that a young person will become violent. Although risk factors contribute to youth violence outcomes, they are not direct causes of youth violence. Several risk factors and four distinct areas or domains in which particular generic traditional risk factors are nested:

(1) risk factors related directly to the individual;

(2) risk factors generated by family;

(3) peer/school risk factors; and

(4) community risk factors.

I maintain that there are macro-structural risk factors that influence youth violence which can represent a fifth domain, and still others contend that there are cultural aspects associated with the Black community that can also be considered as risk factors specifically pertaining to African American young men. The risk factors associated with the macro-structural domain, are not considered as generic traditional risk factors, although, from an isolated perspective, some are listed as community risk factors, with the alluded to perception that structural issues or problems are not the cause of the various deficits that a community may possess, but instead the deficits are a result of a community that is morally defective. And similarly, risk factors associated with the cultural domain are not considered as traditional risk factors. Through my examination of the youth violence literature, I contend that many risk factors for youth violence transcend their categorical domains, integrating into other domains with the effect of influencing, mediating, and interacting with other risk factors.

For the individual, shortfalls in the development of social and emotional competencies may lead to factors associated with violent behavior such as bullying, poor decision making, impulsivity, hyperactivity, involvement with drugs and alcohol, poor behavioral control, and antisocial beliefs and attitudes. Poor family functioning can be linked to risk factors that include: domestic violence; harsh, lax, or inconsistent discipline; parental substance abuse or criminality; low parental education and income; unemployment and underemployment; and poor and/or detrimental relationships between child and parent/ caregiver.

Risk factors related to a child's peer associations include associations with delinquent peers, involvement with youth gangs, or social rejection by peers. A tenuous relationship between the child and their school environment can foster risk factors of poor academic performance, low commitment to school, school failure, and school dropout. In the community, social disorganization as a risk factor may be the breeding ground for other risk factors such as poverty, high turnover of residents, large proportions of disrupted or single-parent families, economic decline, exposure to violent adults and youth gangs, and the presence of crime and drugs. The macro-structural risk factors encompass most of the so-called community risk factors.

The presence and proliferation of crime, drugs, poverty, economic decline, joblessness, racial discrimination, marginalization that leads to alienation, mistrust of police, and hopelessness are not risk factors that exist in a vacuum of community characteristics but are indeed the result of social structure and policy that has underpinnings that include institutionalized racism, capitalistic exploitation, the myth of white supremacy, white privilege, and cultural imperialism. It is a social structure that has historically demeaned, denigrated, degraded, and devalued African American life with special scrutinizing and incriminating attention paid to young Black males. I beleive that the negative outcomes associated with macro-structural deficiencies are subject to cultural adaptations by members of the Black community that substantially increase the risk for violence by African American male youth.

How Some Traditional Risk Factors are Associated with Youth Violence

Although there are individual characteristics and behaviors that put youths more at risk for youth violence, I am very hesitant and reluctant to acquiesce to the labeling of the so-called "individual domain" for youth violence risk factors, even though it identified and categorized some characteristics specific to individuals that may lead to youth violence. I would emphasize however that what has been deemed as individual risk factors do not develop in a void, as if a developing child is not greatly influenced by social and environmental factors, and substantially influenced by their parents in ways that greatly affect their development. The developmental competencies of minority children may be adversely affected by the interaction of other variables of which the aforementioned are included.

An important consideration in the examination of African American male youth violence is the perception by African American youth themselves of the violence and the risk factors that influence violence. An ethnographic approach utilizing focus groups was implemented to explore participants' perceptions of risk factors for violence. Interpretation of the data suggests that many of the perceptions that the participants had were consistent with the traditional risk factors identified in the youth violence prevention literature. From interpretations of the data, participants acknowledged individual risk factors such as a poor self-concept and decision-making as well as the absence of a positive future orientation. They also identified the ability of peers to influence behaviors, particularly in the absence of positive and supportive family relationships. Community characteristics such as poverty, the presence of drugs and gangs were also perceived by them as risk factors for youth violence.

Male individuals have a perception about how acts of delinquency were encouraged and reinforced by some youth in their community, and nonviolence was not socially accepted by some of their peers. The issue of what it meant to be a "man" was associated with aggression. Walking away from confrontations or escalating situations was not viewed as manly by boys due to concerns about being perceived as weak and consequently being teased or bullied by peers. Youth often felt pressure to make choices that essentially traded one risk status for another. The need for social support and acceptance as well as concerns about personal safety may draw a young person towards a gang in spite of the negative perceptions of the gang. It must be noted here that at this young age, the perceptions of these children are mirror images of the perceptions held by older adolescents and young men that have adopted the "Code of the Street" persona that regulates the use of violence in many Black communities. Having an awareness of risk factors for youth violence does not necessarily translate into the resources, skills, desire, and ability to avoid youth violence.

Everyday, African American children face an enormous challenge in negotiating the social and structural environment in which they live. Unfortunately for the African American young men, their perception of what it means to be a man was in direct conflict with their perception that aggression and escalation of conflict increase the risks of violent outcomes. Critical race theorists would suggest that the ubiquitous nature of racism throughout our social institutions help to confound our children's perceptions, and that the structure of society may be an incubator for circumstances that are influencing these contradictory perceptive results.

For African American young men, perceptions are also critical when it comes to the question of respect. The perceived lack of respect by African American male youth may be a risk factor for violence. The the level of respect an African American male youth experiences is directly related to his sense of psychological wellness, social identity, and is critical for his safety, recognition and acceptance. A lack of respect may be perceived by young African American males as a threat to their safety and may spur acts of violence. The perceptions of non-incarcerated youth and incarcerated youth alike, non incarcerated youth were more likely to receive respect from society than incarcerated youth. And not surprisingly because incarcerated youth receive less perceived societal respect, they were reported to be more likely to use violence when their perceptions indicated that they were disrespected. Black youth's perceptions concerning the importance of respect, and how from their worldview perspective, they feel obligated to violently respond when they perceive that someone has disrespected them.

In many instances African American male youth's perceived lack of respect may result in impulsively responding violently to their perceptions. The violent behavioral outcomes that may result from impulsive reactions are real whether the disrespect is actual or perceived. For this reason and others, impulsive behavior is seen as an important risk factor for youth violence. The aggressive impulses are translated into violent actions through the depletion of trait self-control or the existence of already low levels of trait self-control. Results indicated that participants low in trait self-control were particularly likely to express intentions of impulsively behaving aggressively in response to provocation, whereas participants high in self-control did not express impulsive intentions of responding aggressively. The ability to prevent impulsive aggression through trait self-control is diminished when stored self-control has been expended in provocative situations, with those already with lower trait self-control being more likely to show impulsive aggression when they are provoked. The impulsivity was associated with poor self-control that led to aggressive and delinquent behavior among pre-adolescent and early adolescent boys. It is concluded that individual differences in trait self-control predicted impulsivity, rates of violent behavioral problems, and violent criminality over long periods of time.

In relationship to violent criminality over time are various neighborhoods' violent incident and prevalence rates that increases children's exposure to violence, either as victims or witnesses, which is thought to have an influence on their propensity to engage in future violence.

The effects of exposure to violence on adolescents. The Black males have witnessed the most violence and that Black males were also more likely to be victimized by violence than females. In both waves the findings indicated that exposure to violence was closely associated with adolescents' externalizing behaviors. African American male youth exposure to violence was substantially associated with their aggressive and overt antisocial behaviors. When assessed for aggressive behavior as a result of exposure to violence, African American male youth were more likely to exhibit aggressive behavior when compared to females and Whites.

In this society, aggressive behavior is repeatedly linked to the selling and use of drugs that many times result in violent outcomes, especially in urban areas where most of the drug dealers are African American and Latino youth. Drug and substance use/abuse is also psychologically related to a person's desire to relieve anxiety or stress and that adolescents who experience high levels of environmental stress are more likely to use alcohol or drugs. Stress is related to behavioral problems in young African Americans males because of increased exposure to prejudice, discrimination, and hostility. They indicate that "life event" stress in African American youth was related to behavior problems for boys without any moderation by locus of control, family environment, social support, or coping style. African American adolescents who participated in all five waves of a school dropout and drug use. Their findings indicated that 40% of the youth were chronically stressed or showed an increasing level of stress over time. It was found that African American adolescents with high or increasing levels of stress during high school had exhibited more antisocial behaviors in ninth grade than youth with low levels of stress.

The early delinquency in African American adolescents is significantly related to high or increasing levels of stress. Seen as operating in a closed positive system, stress appears to be mediated by many of the risk factors for violent antisocial deviant behaviors while at the same time it is also exacerbating the activation of those same risk factor mediators. African American youth suffering from high levels of chronic and/or increasing stress enhances the possibility for them to engage in some form of violent antisocial behavior.

Role of Racism-Related Social Support

In my opinion, racism-related social support moderated the relationship between the experience of racial discrimination and depression. By contrast, racism-related social support positively influenced psychological well-being but did not moderate the effect of racism on psychological well-being. That is, the negative effect of racism on psychological well-being is similar for individuals who reported different levels of perceived racism-related social support. There are several possible reasons for the differential findings. To better explain such different findings, it should continue to examine the effects of both general and specific social support in affecting the relationship between stress and distress/well-being. There are several models regarding the role of social support. Therefore, a person who feels someone is there to support him/her in stressful situations is likely to have a high level of psychological well-being, even though such perceived availability of support may not cancel out undesirable effects of stressful events.

Theoretical Implications

New perspectives regarding the effects of racism on African American children's well-being and mental health. First, it adds new elements (i.e., psychological well-being) to the "bio psychosocial model", which describes various potential mediators and moderators that could affect the racism-health relationship. Some dimensions of psychological well-being (such as mastery) as mediators between discrimination and distress, the role of overall psychological well-being using a longitudinal analysis examining change in distress over time.

Second, it provides support to the literature demonstrating individual resilience as well as vulnerability following traumatic experiences. Although painful and harmful to one's level of mastery, stressful events may facilitate individuals' growth. However, in general, stress would lead to impaired psychological well-being which in turn causes mental suffering. Third, racism-related social support was not found to moderate the effect of racism on psychological well-being. Instead, such support had a direct positive effect on psychological well-being. This may provide new insights into the role of situation-specific support as it relates to psychological well-being.

Finally, the environmental mastery and personal growth dimensions of psychological well-being may be uniquely related to perceived discrimination. There are controversies regarding whether psychological well-being has as many as six dimensions. Researchers have insisted that the six-factor model is valid both theoretically and statistically, but there is overlap among the dimensions. If the six dimensions have unique characteristics net of their shared "overall psychological well-being" component, then they should be uniquely related to other constructs and thereby demonstrate discriminant validity. That is, each dimension should have some component or components that are not shared by the other dimensions. The perceived racism did uniquely affect the environmental mastery and personal growth dimensions of psychological well-being, providing evidence of the two-level structure of the psychological well-being construct. On the other hand, all six dimensions of psychological well-being do not seem to be uniquely predictive of psychological distress.

It is important that children of all cultures be respected and given every opportunity to live a healthy and productive life. Free from violence, hate, prejudice, racism, and evil. Only then can we truly say that children of the world will live out their life's in a productive and healthy manner.

<u>Let Our Children Live</u>

<u>The End</u>

INDEX

Please note any and all definition of terms, theories, concept, ideologies, projects discussed in this book, postulates, and research contributors. Are all defined and given credit for contributions made in each area within this book.

GLOSSARY

Please note that all definitions of terms, within the context of this book. Are defined for the readers understanding, within the context of this book.